O's

Little Book of
Calm & Comfort

Other Titles in O's Little Books Series

O's

Little Book of
Calm & Comfort

The Editors of O, *The Oprah Magazine*

FLATIRON
BOOKS
NEW YORK

www.flatironbooks.com

The Library of Congress Cataloging-in-Publication Data
is available upon request.

ISBN 978-1-250-07008-1 (hardcover)
ISBN 978-1-250-07009-8 (e-book)

Our books may be purchased in bulk for promotional, educational,
or business use. Please contact your local bookseller or the Macmillan
Corporate and Premium Sales Department at 1-800-221-7945, extension
5442, or by e-mail at MacmillanSpecialMarkets@macmillan.com.

First Edition: March 2017

10 9 8 7 6 5 4 3

In the best of times and worst of times,
I know for sure, this life is a gift.

—Oprah Winfrey

Contents

Simple Solace

"Dear old world," she murmured, "you are very lovely, and I am glad to be alive in you."

—LUCY MAUD MONTGOMERY,
ANNE OF GREEN GABLES

Ride It Out

Robin Romm

I come from a long line of worriers. It's in my blood. My grandfather Sam fretted ceaselessly—about money, security, status, the future of his only granddaughter. When I quit my government job (with its regular hours, pay raises, and benefits) to pursue a creative writing degree, Sam, who'd lived through the Depression, clutched at his balding head and wailed. When I broke up with my Jewish boyfriend before he went to law school, Sam nearly collapsed in grief. When I decided to buy a one-hundred-year-old house, he howled, "What about the roof? What will you do about the *roof*?"

In truth, that stressed me out, too. I didn't want to end up like Sam, though—who, despite all his worry (meant, presumably, to keep crisis at bay), was never able to find peace. So I always did my best to push my anxieties aside. But a few years ago, after my mother died and I lost a big job, anxiety nearly overwhelmed me. I tried exercise, relaxation tapes, therapy, time with my dog, time with friends, time with Xanax. They helped, but on my worst days, I found myself clinging to the life raft of worry.

Then I was accepted to an artist's residency that happened to be at a dude ranch in Wyoming. I had gone horseback riding a few times as a kid, though never with any seriousness. ("Horses!" I can imagine Sam screeching, shaking his head so hard bits of spittle would fly. "You would have to be out of your mind!") But after two weeks of watching the horses and wishing the artists were allowed to ride them, I managed to beg my way onto one. Never mind that it was only a trail ride and I had terrible form (I slumped in the saddle and threw my weight around awkwardly)—I felt something stirring in my gut. On horseback, the stronghold of my worries loosened, because I was moving so fast I couldn't think. I could only feel: the animal running, the sky touching my face, the wind in my hair. It felt like a release. It felt right.

When I returned home to Oregon after the residency, I

found a barn and a trainer (upbeat, not at all anxious), and before long, I was cantering bareback and learning to train troubled horses. My favorite is a retired Thoroughbred named Jake, a chestnut gelding with liquid Disney eyes. Jake can move fast, and when he does, I feel myself slide into myself, like a penny into a slot. I lean in and that horse keeps going, faster and faster, until he's practically flying and I am totally unthinking. I am simply there.

"You are going to break your neck!" I can hear Sam warn. But I can't worry about that. Worry isn't safe. In fact, at the barn, where horses spook at the first signs of trouble, worry shows itself for what it is: a liability. Horses value calm above all other virtues. I'm new to their world, but it turns out I share their values.

A Circle of Arms

Tracy Young

After our mother died, my younger sisters and I began what would become a tradition: an annual get-together, just the four of us, no spouses, no kids. It would be a chance, although no one ever came out and said as much, to talk about what had happened. And we did, haltingly, spiking the conversation with the edgy jokes that are our family vernacular. But the conversation was less important than the gathering itself, the warm huddle of beings who had known one another their entire lives. Eventually, our reunions became less an observance and more an adventure. We started taking trips—most recently to a spa in Vermont, where we also celebrated my sister Susie's birthday.

It was a happy occasion and we indulged ourselves accordingly, springing for exotic forms of massage, hiking in the woods, and eating our favorite candy. In real life, we were all middle-aged women; here we were just, well, sisters. Laughing, goofing on waiters, dishing about old friends, until the conversation turned, inevitably, to each of our unhappy adolescences.

I was telling my sisters about a time—I must have been around twenty, living at home between reckless bouts of the sixties—when I was freaking out over something. What? I have no clear recollection except that of feeling lost. But I do remember trailing my mother into the bathroom and sitting on the toilet seat to watch her as she put on her lipstick with her little collapsible brush, preparing to go out for the evening. I felt about four years old. And I remember wishing—the voice so loud in my head I was sure she could hear it—that she would come over and put her arms around me. I didn't say so. Our family was not expressive in that way. And at that particular moment, either I didn't think my mother would understand or I didn't want to tell her what was wrong. I wanted something words could not express. I just wanted a hug.

"Oh my God," said Susie. "That's exactly what Robin said to me." Robin, her daughter, was now about the age I'd been back then and had been fighting her own demons—until somehow she seemed to right herself, like a small skiff in a big sea. "She said that when she was in trouble, what she really needed was for me to give her a hug," Susie said. "And I had no idea."

"Well," I said, "at least you know now."

There was more to say. About missed opportunities and our strange broken legacy. But instead we ate some strawberry Twizzlers and started a hilarious pantomime, a sign language for freaking out (fingers clenched as if holding onto a cliff—the fewer the fingers, the more dire the freakout) and a sign (arms encircled, then a little wave) that meant, *I'm sending you a hug.*

During the eight thousand years I spent in therapy learning to express the feelings that were forbidden in my family, there were days when I sat on the couch shredding Kleenex while my therapist looked at me with compassion and I wished I could crawl into her lap. At times like these, it struck me that psychotherapy was too much work and too little comfort. Naming my most primitive feelings seemed a gratingly cerebral approach to what were almost physical sensations. Words, no matter how well-intentioned, bounced off me like hail.

None of which is to say that I harbor many illusions that a hug could have changed my life. Or anyone's. (I grew up near a large Italian clan to whose house I would flee when I craved the noise and heat of another kind of family, where the mother, a former masseuse, was a hugger without peer. They all turned out to be crazy as bedbugs.) But in the moment, I have no doubt, a hug can ground you. Pull you back from the edge. Or out of your head. Into a circle of arms and the sturdy comforts of the present.

"Language is a skin," wrote Roland Barthes in *A Lover's Discourse*. And so is skin a language. It speaks when words fail us and communicates to parts of ourselves that are beyond the reach of words. The simple fact is that we are, first and foremost, mammals. We thrive on touch. Grooming is part of our social behavior, which may explain the relationship we have with our hairdressers. (A friend once asked her shrink, "Is it a love problem or a hair problem?" "I think it's a hair problem," he said.)

I'm still easily put off by indiscriminate hugging. But I

can be moved to tears watching baseball, when the batter rounds third, races down the baseline, and the entire dugout charges out to embrace him. Granted, it's an occasion of triumph, not tragedy. But the message is the same. You're one of us! it says. You're home.

Junk

Aimee Bender

The jagged piece of red taillight that I fished from the trunk of my first car before I sold it; the tiny burgundy wooden elephant that holds a thousand tinier paper elephants that I ordered from a toy catalog when I was seven; a bottle of facial spray from a friend that's still full; the gray rock, from an Encinitas beach, that my college boyfriend gave me, and a few rocks from various other beaches whose significance I can't recall: My junk drawer holds uncategorizable items that only I can decipher, and even I'm not sure I can decipher all of them anymore.

My grandmother had a secret drawer in her bedroom, and when we visited, she allowed us to fish in it with our eyes closed and pick a treasure for the day from among the pens, plastic animals, and candy bars. One of my best finds was an empty smoky-rose glass Estée Lauder moisturizer jar with a gold lid, bulby and beautiful. I held it close all day and later gave a small doll a bath in it. My junk drawer has the same aura of mystery, and though I don't fish in it, I do open it from time to time just to pick up the items inside and look at them. I like that they are both meaningful and meaningless. Even though I have to tightly cram envelopes and other useful things in the drawers that surround it, I keep my junk drawer protected.

I believe in a space that has no designated purpose and yet some reason for existence. I believe that every clean house needs a chaotic spot. I believe in places where we can go to marvel at the unknowable intricacies of our minds.

Splendor on the Couch

Nora Ephron

I've just surfaced from spending several days in a state of rapture: I was reading a book. I loved this book. I loved every second of it. I was transported into its world. I was reminded of all sorts of things in my own life. I was in anguish over the fate of its characters. I felt alive and engaged and positively brilliant, bursting with ideas, brimming with memories of other books I've loved. I composed a dozen imaginary letters to the author, letters I'll never actually, physically write, much less send—letters of praise, letters of entirely inappropriate information about my own experiences with the author's subject matter, even a letter of recrimination when one of the characters died and I was grief-stricken. But mostly I composed imaginary letters of gratitude: The state of rapture that occurs when I read a wonderful book is one of the main reasons I read, but it doesn't happen every time, or even every other time, and when it does, I'm truly beside myself with joy.

When I was a child, nearly every book sent me into something approaching bliss. Can I be romanticizing my early reading experiences? I don't think so. I can tick off so many books that I read and reread when I was growing up—foremost among them the Oz books, which I was obsessed with—but so many others that were favorites in the most compelling way. I wanted so badly to be Jane Banks, growing up in London with Mary Poppins for a nanny, or Homer Price, growing up in Centerburg with an uncle who owned a doughnut machine that wouldn't stop making doughnuts. Little Sara Crewe in Frances Hodgson Burnett's classic *A Little Princess* was my alter ego—not in any real way, you understand, as she was a much better-behaved child than I ever was, but I was so entranced by the story of the little rich girl who was sent up to the garret to be the scullery maid at the fancy boarding school where she'd been a pampered student before her father died. Oh, how I wanted to be an orphan! I read *The Nun's Story,* and oh, how I wanted to be a nun! I wanted to be shipwrecked on a desert island and stranded in Krakatoa! I wanted to be Ozma and Jo March and Anne Frank and Nancy Drew and Eloise and Anne of Green Gables—and what's more, I could be, at least in my imagination.

Here's a strange thing: Whenever I read a book I love, I start to remember all the others that I fell in love with, and I can remember where I was living and the couch I was sitting on when I read them. After college, in Greenwich Village, I sat on my brand-new wide-wale-corduroy couch and read *The Golden Notebook* by Doris Lessing, the extraordinary novel that changed my life and the lives of so many other young women in the 1960s. I have the paperback copy I read at the time, and it's dog-eared, epiphany after epiphany marked so that I could easily refer back to them. Does anyone read *The Golden Notebook* nowadays? I don't know, but back then, just before the second stage of the women's movement burst into being, I was electrified by Lessing's heroine, Anna, and her struggle to become a free woman. Work, friendship, love, sex, politics, psychoanalysis, writing—all the things that preoccupied me were Lessing's subjects, and I can remember how many times I put the book down, reeling from its brilliance and insights.

Cut to a few years later. The couch is covered with a purple slipcover, and I'm reading for pure pleasure—it's *The Godfather* by Mario Puzo, a divine book that sweeps me off into a wave of romantic delirium. I want to be a mafioso! No, that's not quite right. Okay then, I want to be a mafioso's wife! No, that's not quite right either. Okay then, I'd rather be married to Michael Corleone than married to the man I happen to be married to. Exclamation point.

A few years later, I'm divorced. No surprise. The couch and I have moved to a dark apartment in the West Fifties. It's a summer weekend, I have nothing whatsoever to do, and I should be lonely, but I'm not—I'm reading the collected works of Raymond Chandler. Six years later, another divorce: For weeks I've been unable to focus, to settle down, to read anything at all. A friend I'm staying with gives me the bound galleys of *Smiley's People.* I sink into bed and happily surrender to John Le Carré. I love John Le Carré, but I'm even more in love with his hero, George Smiley, the spy with the broken heart. I want George Smiley to get over his broken heart. I want him to get over his horrible ex-wife who betrayed him. I want George Smiley to fall in love. I want George Smiley to fall in love with me. George Smiley, come to think of it, is exactly the sort of person I ought to marry and never do. I make a mental note to write Le Carré a letter giving him the benefit of my wisdom on this score.

But meanwhile, my purple couch is lost in the divorce and I buy a new couch, a wonderful squishy thing covered with a warm, cozy fabric, with arms you can lie back on and cushions you can sink into. On it I read most of Anthony Trollope and all of Edith Wharton, both of whom are dead and can't be written to. Too bad: I'd like to tell them their books are as contemporary as they were when they were written. I read all of Jane Austen, six novels back-to-back, and spend days blissfully worrying over whether the lovers in each book will ever overcome the misunderstandings, objections, misapprehensions, character flaws, class distinctions, and all the other obstacles to love. I read these novels in a state of suspense so intense that you would never guess I have read them all at least ten times before.

And finally, one day I read the book that is probably the most rapturous book of my adult life. On a chaise longue at the beach on a beautiful summer day, I open Wilkie Collins's masterpiece, *The Woman in White*, probably the first great work of mystery fiction ever written (although that description hardly does it justice), and I am instantly lost to the world. Days pass as I savor every word. Each minute I spend away from the book pretending to be interested in everyday life is a misery. How could I have waited so long to read this book? When can I get back to it? Halfway through I return to New York to work on a movie, and I sit in the studio unable to focus on anything but whether my favorite character in the book will survive. I will not be able to bear it if anything bad happens to my beloved Marian Halcombe. Every so often I look up from the book and see a roomful of people waiting for me to make a decision about whether the music is too soft or the thunder is too loud, and I can't believe they don't understand that what I'm doing is much more important—I'm reading the most wonderful book.

There's something called the rapture of the deep, and it refers to what happens when a deep-sea diver spends too much time at the bottom of the ocean and can't tell which way is up. When he surfaces he's liable to have a condition called the bends, where the body can't adapt to the oxygen levels in the atmosphere. All this happens to me when I resurface from a book. The book I'm currently resurfacing from is *The Amazing Adventures of Kavalier & Clay* by

Michael Chabon. It's about two men who create comic book characters—but it's also about how artists create magical things from the events of everyday life. At one point the book's hero sees a roomful of moths, and then a huge luna moth sitting in a maple tree in Union Square Park; a few pages later, he reinvents what he's seen by creating a fabulous comic book heroine named Luna Moth. The moment Luna Moth flew into the novel was so breathtaking that I had to put down the book. I was almost dazed by the playfulness of the author and his ability to do something so difficult with such apparent ease. Chabon's novel takes place in New York City in the 1940s, and though I finished reading it more than a week ago, I'm still there. I'm smoking Camels, and Salvador Dalí is at a party in the next room. Eventually, I'll have to start breathing the air in modern-day New York again, but on the other hand, perhaps I won't. I'll find another book I love and disappear into it. Wish me luck.

Gratitude

Robin Wall Kimmerer

On an April morning, my corner of the earth fairly thrums with music: Robins sing from treetops, peepers call from the pond, and the maple sap plinks as it drops into buckets. I remember how when my daughters were small, they would wrap their little arms around the trees and catch the sap on their tongues. I believe that in the same way, we all must fully embrace the wonder of the earth, a planet that provides us with everything we need. Sometimes I'm nearly overwhelmed by the deluge of gifts Earth bestows on us, entirely unearned: water, air, food, the ground beneath our feet. The very things that keep us alive.

So what should be our response to the generosity of the world? Paying attention to it. Drinking it in. Letting its energy flow into us. Celebrating all the experiences we have here—the physical and spiritual things, the tranquil and exhilarating things, prayer and poetry and pancakes alike. And then repaying Earth with our gratitude. That robin sings her thanks at sunrise every morning. Ask yourself, "What do I do to say thanks?" Ask yourself, "Am I living in a way that the earth can be grateful for me?" We can share our human gifts—of art, of science, of action, of fierce defense for the good green world. And most of all, we can share our awe.

Welcome to Your Body

Amy Maclin

So many of us have never fully settled into our bodies. We inhabit them as an afterthought, the way we might live in a rented room. And the accommodations are rarely up to our standards: At thirteen, we wonder whether we'll ever grow breasts; at thirty, we lament our swimsuited lumpiness; at fifty, we look at pictures of ourselves at thirty and can't believe we ever had it so good.

With all the drama surrounding the way our bodies look, we too rarely think of the things they do. Or, for that matter, all the things they *are*. Our bodies are the protagonists of our most momentous stories—they lie with our lovers, birth our babies, walk us forward into each day. They are the physical manifestation of our emotions.

They're also philanthropists, giving endlessly to meet needs we don't even realize we have. On a hot afternoon, your finely calibrated thermoregulatory system produces sweat to keep you from overheating. As you eat and drink, saliva protects your tooth enamel by bathing it in calcium and other minerals. When your bladder is almost full, receptors in its wall send messages to the spinal cord, setting off a chain of signals that will eventually prompt you to take a bathroom break. Every day a host of benevolent mysteries is happening inside you.

And there's good reason to ponder them: Being more in tune with your body can help you feel better about it. In one study, researchers at Royal Holloway, University of London, asked female subjects to silently count their heartbeats without feeling their pulse. The ones who judged more accurately—who had more "interoceptive awareness," or a sense of their own physiology—were less likely to think of their body as a mere object and more likely to judge it based on competence than appearance. According to some researchers, women who "self-objectify," who see their physical being only as something to look at and evaluate, are more prone to depression, eating disorders, and sexual dysfunction.

Living in a body brings its share of challenges, but our mortal flesh is capable of amazing feats. (To name a few: defying gravity, sensing danger, telling stories, and carrying around our souls.) So next time you're about to tell yourself how big your butt looks in those pants, try listening to your heart instead.

Futzing

Lise Funderburg

What gladdens my perfection-obsessed heart is to attempt projects that don't matter, at least not in the grand scheme of things. So I make Pinterest-inspired marshmallow snowmen sliding down a coconut cake on fruit-leather toboggans for a five-year-old's birthday, and neither of us cares that their sugar-sprinkle eyes dribble down to their chins. I watch videos of men chiseling rocks in the English countryside and then go out to lay my own stone wall, half of which survives. The whole while, I forsake doing things flawlessly and instead just do them—for the joy of learning something new, for the pleasure of thinking with my hands, for the sweet delight of merely trying.

Send, Receive

Kristy Davis

When my mom died, we bought electronics.

My father sat across from me in a restaurant booth. Here was a man I hardly recognized: vulnerable. Two days before, cancer had killed my mom in the bedroom they had shared for almost thirty years.

"So how's school going?" he asked.

"Fine," I said.

"You know, your mother wanted you to go."

"I know, Dad."

I've heard my father—a retired air force colonel, devoted Christian, and family patriarch—compared to the Paul Newman character Cool Hand Luke, a prisoner whose bulletproof resolve leads to trouble. Obstinacy isn't my father's only flaw, though. In the words of one of that film's characters, "What we've got here is failure to communicate." And I'm every bit as guilty as my dad.

Because we couldn't talk about God, politics, or her, we went to Best Buy. We trolled the fluorescent aisles, browsing among the shiny objects. It smelled like plastic. It sounded like static. Talking about operating systems counts as a weighty conversation between my father and me. The man owns his own power generator, fiber-optic flashlight, and solar-powered radio. I've had my obsessive phases, too: rock climbing, photography, lighting design equipment. We are a lot alike. We are completely opposite. I'm Apple, he's PC.

As my mother lay dying, my father upgraded every device he could think of; in the days after her death, he and I spent a lot of time getting them to work. While my brothers transported family members, and my sisters went to the morgue, he and I saw to all things technical. We hardly had time for condolences.

"Computer stuff," my older brother said when someone asked after our whereabouts. "They're in there doing computer stuff."

In the week between her death and the funeral, we went on another binge. My dad bought two keyboards (one collapsible, one hardwired) for his new laptop and a wireless mouse and modem. We had a lot of work to do, a service to plan. We needed all systems up and running. We threw ourselves into the technical part of things with single-minded zeal. Every hour brought some new urgent necessity: USB cables, another modem, better software, photo paper, ink cartridges.

My older sister created a PowerPoint presentation featuring family photographs set to a ukulele player's rendition of "Over the Rainbow." We bought an LCD projector to display the slide show. I drove an hour south to buy a mini disc player to record the service. It wasn't enough to turn on an analog tape recorder. We needed top-quality sound, good enough for a movie.

I hadn't been able to help my mother as she keened with pain. I had stared at the white wall, bawling, until my sister (a nurse who was doing all the work anyway) mercifully asked me to get something from the other room. But I could set up the laptop near my mother's bed, in case she wanted to do any typing. My father could buy stuff, then figure it out. He could get wireless Internet for a family of laptops. He could be useful, in his way.

The funeral went off without a hitch. But still we bought more: a large television that, through its connection to the phone, told us who was calling; a light box for seasonal affective disorder; a clock that projected the time onto the bedroom ceiling. My purchases were funded in part with money from my mother's life insurance. After the cash ran out, I felt better: From the start, it hadn't been a fair trade.

Our behavior was so obvious, my father's and mine. We'd flicked the off switch on our grief box. Why couldn't we look each other in the eye and say, "The person who loved us most, and whom we loved most, is gone"?

Maybe that would have felt cheap. Maybe we couldn't have told the truth, even if we had tried. Maybe we would have just obscured each other with saccharine sayings and a dose of God.

And what *is* the truth?

That death changed us.

Recently we've begun exchanging e-mails. My father wrote—and this is something I've never heard him say— "Always remember; my love for you is not conditional.... I love you because you are my lovely daughter, and nothing can ever change that."

At the moment of crisis, he and I were workers in our small electronic hive, busy little bees attending to everything but the crisis itself. We were documentarians, resurrecting the dead in high-def. We were doing what we could. We were learning how to be capable of more.

This Little Light of Yours

Elizabeth Gilbert

Some years ago, I was stuck on a crosstown bus in New York City during rush hour. Traffic was barely moving. The bus was filled with cold, tired people who were deeply irritated—with one another; with the rainy, sleety weather; with the world itself. Two men barked at each other about a shove that might or might not have been intentional. A pregnant woman got on, and nobody offered her a seat. Rage was in the air; no mercy would be found here.

But as the bus approached Seventh Avenue, the driver got on the intercom. "Folks," he said, "I know you've had a rough day and you're frustrated. I can't do anything about the weather or traffic, but here's what I can do. As each one of you gets off the bus, I will reach out my hand to you. As you walk by, drop your troubles into the palm of my hand, okay? Don't take your problems home to your families tonight—just leave 'em with me. My route goes right by the Hudson River, and when I drive by there later, I'll open the window and throw your troubles in the water. Sound good?"

It was as if a spell had lifted. Everyone burst out laughing. Faces gleamed with surprised delight. People who'd been pretending for the past hour not to notice each other's existence were suddenly grinning at each other like, Is this guy serious?

Oh, he was serious.

At the next stop—just as he had promised—the driver reached out his hand, palm up, and waited. One by one, all the exiting commuters placed their hand just above his and mimed the gesture of dropping something into his palm. Some people laughed as they did this, some teared up—but everyone did it. The driver repeated the same lovely ritual at the next stop, too. And the next. All the way to the river.

We live in a hard world, my friends. Sometimes it's extra difficult to be a human being. Sometimes you have a bad day. Sometimes you have a bad day that lasts for several years. You struggle and fail. You lose jobs, money, friends, faith, and love. You witness horrible events unfolding in the news, and you become fearful and withdrawn. There are times when everything seems cloaked in darkness. You long for the light but don't know where to find it.

But what if *you* are the light? What if you're the very agent of illumination that a dark situation begs for?

That's what this bus driver taught me—that anyone can be the light, at any moment. This guy wasn't some big power player. He wasn't a spiritual leader. He wasn't some media-savvy "influencer." He was a bus driver—one of society's most invisible workers. But he possessed real power, and he used it beautifully for our benefit.

When life feels especially grim, or when I feel particularly powerless in the face of the world's troubles, I think of this man and ask myself, What can I do, right now, to be the light? Of course, I can't personally end all wars, or solve global warming, or transform vexing people into entirely different creatures. I definitely can't control traffic. But I do have some influence on everyone I brush up against, even if we never speak or learn each other's names. How we behave matters, because within human society everything is contagious—sadness and anger, yes, but also patience and generosity. Which means we all have more influence than we realize.

No matter who you are, or where you are, or how mundane or tough your situation may seem, I believe you can illuminate your world. In fact, I believe this is the only way the world will ever be illuminated—one bright act of grace at a time, all the way to the river.

Laugh It Off

Ian Frazier

The tap water hits a spoon in the sink and sprays you. You pull a window shade and it just keeps going and going. You can't roll up a garden hose in any dignified way. You have to become a connoisseur of these events—*Wow, look at that, that's great*. You have to hope that a higher power is saying, *That was a good one!* And that you're sharing the divine pleasure it's taking in your misfortune.

Thanks, Birdy

Catherine Newman

Birdy, my seven-year-old daughter, was sitting on my lap
in yet another doctor's office, cracking herself up about a
recent Halloween party. "Remember that kid dressed up
as a corpse?" she asked. "I thought he was going to look
like trail mix. But when I saw him in those gross sheets, I
realized I was thinking of gorp!" Her loony, snorting laugh
echoed throughout the waiting room.

A few months earlier, while slathering Birdy with sun-
screen, I'd discovered a lump on her torso. And so began
a marathon diagnostic relay as she was handed off from
this specialist to that pediatric expert like a pigtailed
baton. On medical charts, the lump was described as a
"mass in the chest wall," and I felt like I had one, too—my

heart knotted in preemptive grief. There were X-rays, ultrasounds, and a harrowing MRI, all to determine the substance and intentions of this mass. Bone? Soft tissue? Benign cyst? Malignant tumor? My fear of losing Birdy was like a deafening drumbeat that drowned out everything, including reason.

Then, sitting in that doctor's office, I heard her laugh, and somehow her cheer rang through, reminding me: There is this. There's really only ever this. In that moment, I realized I could terrify myself, imagining a future with no Birdy, or I could pine for the carefree, lump-free Birdy of the past—or I could be present for the real girl who was right in front of me, and pay attention as her cheerfully unraveling braids bobbed against me and her little body shook with mirth. There were the hands that petted our cat as gently as you'd touch a soap bubble; there was the gap-toothed smile that made her look like a strangely radiant old man. When I promised her an ice-cream cone after yet another sonogram, she couldn't believe her good fortune. Her energy reminded me that life isn't about avoiding trouble; it's about being present, even through the hard stuff, so you don't miss the very thing you're trying not to lose.

After two more months of loony, snorting laughter in waiting rooms—reading *Amos & Boris* together, me looking into her pink-cheeked little face—the doctors decided that Birdy's lump was just an enthusiastic growth of cartilage. Can you imagine the relief? Of course you can. You've had dark, scary times, too—the times you were sure you were losing your job, your friend, your love, your mind. And maybe through it all, you already knew that this moment is all we have. Me, I needed to learn it from Birdy.

Kindred Spirits

To get the full value of a joy you must have
somebody to divide it with.

—MARK TWAIN

Love and Weirdness

Liza Monroy

My confession: I'm a thirty-four-year-old woman who is addicted to a Nintendo race-car game called *Mario Kart 8.* In the game there are thirty-two tracks you can choose from, each with a distinct landscape and cast of characters. My favorite is Shy Guy Falls. It's a crystal mine where the Shy Guys—they look like sea mammals in wizard robes—pickax away at the glittering rocks, chanting a sound I can only describe as *brip-brap, brip-brap, brip-brap.* This sound mesmerizes me.

"Hear them brip-brapping?" I once asked my husband.

"What?" he said, confused.

"Listen."

Brip-brap, brip-brap.

"Huh," he said. "I didn't notice."

Me, I hear the *brip-brap* everywhere—in flip-flops on pavement, in the barking of a dog, in restaurant noise. And out of my own mouth. For months I've been emitting *brip-braps*—at normal speaking volume—as I cook, clean, shop for groceries, eat dinner, hike, work. It's possible that people hear me, but I'm not embarrassed. Brip-brapping is, for me, a centering mantra. Yogis have it all wrong: *Brip-brap*, not *om*, is the rhythm of the universe.

I love *brip-braps* in part because I love those little Shy Guys. But then, I would: They look like otters. God, do I love otters. I'm so in love with them that I bawl whenever I see them in person. I don't fawn and coo—I break into racking sobs. I'm not self-conscious about the tears any more than I am about the *brip-brap*, despite the gawking of bystanders at zoos, aquariums, and beaches. The unleashing of emotion at the sight of my aquatic soul mates is cathartic, a kind of release.

You may be asking, how often is this woman seeing otters? Well, a lot, ever since I moved from New York City to Santa Cruz, California. Here, otters live unconfined. I encounter them nearly as often as I did subway rats back on the East Coast. The first time my then fiancé took me to see the wild otters in the bay, I wept. When he didn't call off the engagement, I knew I'd found the One. (When he gave me *Mario Kart 8* as a surprise gift, I was even more certain.)

The other day, as he and I dragged our kayak down to the ocean, I *brip-brapped* to the beat of our steps, shaking with the excitement of seeing otters. And that was when I had an out-of-body experience, seeing myself as though from above. The person I saw was strange. Like, really strange.

"You sure you won't stop loving me because I'm so weird?" I said.

"That's *why* I love you," he said.

The space that real love makes for weirdness—mine and everyone's—is everything.

That day my husband and I paddled into the kelp beds, the otters' domain, and he joined in the *brip-brap* with me, both of us scanning the ocean's surface for their furry little Shy Guy heads.

Acts of Friendship

Maeve Binchy

I once received a huge, expensive flower arrangement from a person I didn't like, who'd sent it out of pure guilt. It had a hideous bird-of-paradise in the middle and I thought it would never fade and die. I hated it.

Yet the kindness of a friend who will give time and energy, no money involved, will stay with me forever. Like my friend Della, who is a truly great cook. One of her acts of friendship is to invite her less skilled friends to come stay overnight, and then she teaches us to make three knockout meals. She is full of great hints, like don't try to cook the starter or the dessert the day of the dinner; these must be cold or prepared a day ahead so you can concentrate on the main dish with a free heart. You can ask her anything, no matter how silly. Like what does it mean when the directions say, "Cook until ready"—surely the most annoying piece of advice ever given. When is it ready? Is my ready your ready? Or what about "reduce by half"? It can't possibly mean throw half the dish away, so what *does* it mean?

I have another friend who will lend us her ten-year-old son for a morning.

"Show Maeve how to open a computer file and put it in a folder."

"But she *must* know how to do that by now!" he wails, appalled. In his world people are born knowing how to do that.

My friend tells him of stories and novels wandering around in cyberspace because I don't know how to tie them down in my computer. Another week she might send this sterling lad to tune in the television or set the answering machine or download from the digital camera. It's a fabulous gift, so much more welcome than that awful flower arrangement.

I know a woman who hates ironing with a passion, while her neighbor regards it as a peaceful, almost therapeutic thing to do. Every Monday at lunchtime they visit one house or the other. Mary irons eight shirts beautifully; Susie takes silver powder and an old toothbrush and cleans the intricate bits of Mary's silver, making it gleam. One hour and a bowl of soup later, they are happy people with a huge sense of achievement.

I have been blessed with friends who *do* things rather than buy things: friends who will change books at the library, take a bag of your old clothes to a thrift store, bring you cuttings and plant them in a window box, fill the bird feeder in your garden when you're away.

What do I do for friends?

Not enough, but I can help them write difficult letters because I know writing should always be shorter rather than longer and clearer rather than more complicated. I make lists of good movies to watch so they won't be perplexed next time they try to choose one. I take great pictures of them at happy times and send them copies, and I show them how to construct a family tree, which they always end up loving.

Never mind money. The gifts of time and skill call into being the richest marketplace in the world.

Lost and Found

Mary Gaitskill

Last fall I lost my cat Gattino. He was still a kitten, or, at seven months, an adolescent. I had just started letting him outside unsupervised. One day I went away for two hours, and when I came back he was gone. I put flyers everywhere, including in people's mailboxes. I checked shelters and vets. For weeks people reported seeing him; I believed them because Gattino had one blind eye, and in headlights only one of his eyes lit up. Apparently he was quite close by. But I couldn't find him. I couldn't believe he didn't want to come home; it was already quite cold, and he was a fragile cat.

At the same time that this happened, I "lost" two children I'd been involved with for years. I'd met them through the Fresh Air Fund, an organization that facilitates city children coming up to the country to stay for one or two weeks with a rural family to experience animals, nature, and privilege. The two children were from a single-parent, brutally poor household. They were beautiful children, inside and out. They were also emotionally damaged in complicated ways. That didn't matter. I don't have children of my own, and I loved them. We developed a relationship with them that went beyond the organization through which we had been introduced. They came to visit us at Christmas and sometimes their birthdays. I met them in the city on occasion. I sent them books, helped them with their homework, paid for them to go to Catholic school. There were a lot of problems over the years, a lot of tears. Kids who have been treated badly all their lives have difficulty taking in love and a vision of life in which they count, even if they want it. And what we could do was limited. The girl, who was older, got kicked out of school, started running with violent kids, and dropped away from us. I still send her books and talk to her on the phone every now and then. Last year I took her to see a play. But for the moment, anyway, she is gone. The fall that the cat disappeared, the boy began to move away, too. It started with him the same way it started with her; he would spend hours doing his homework with me, and then he would not turn it in. He would come up with a variety of excuses for this. But the real reason was clear: He wanted to fail because it was expected of him, by virtually everyone.

Gattino had been in trouble when I met him, too. I was traveling in Italy when I found him, a tiny, half-starved, sick kitty going blind in both eyes. I didn't intend to take him home with me. I thought I would nurse him to health and then put him back where I found him, where he would at least have a fighting chance. But during the five weeks I spent with him, I got too attached to leave him. He was still sick when it came time to leave (his respiratory illness was chronic) and technically too young to travel— but I moved hell and high water to get him on the plane. I brought him home, and he was incredibly happy to be there with us, and incredibly loving. And then I lost him.

I spent months looking for that cat, hoping against all odds to find him. I didn't. Sometimes I would sit looking out the window with tears running down my face, and I would think, Love is a truly terrible thing. And I have picked the wrong people, and creature, to love.

But when I was out looking for Gattino, sometimes I would think something else. I would think of how brave he was, how intrepid. Like many animals, he had a big heart in his tiny body. During the sixteen-hour trip home from Italy, he didn't cry once. He sat in his carrier gazing at me alertly; he sat in my lap and played with me; he played with the little girl next to me; he would have walked up and down the aisles if he could. No matter what happened to him out in the cold, he would have met it with absolute presence and courage. No matter what, he would have been absolutely himself. That is a kind of love; a kind that doesn't have expectations of how things should be, or how people should be, either. It is a love that respects what is, even if what is involves something terrible for yourself and those you care for. It is very tough and unsentimental; it is also very gentle. It is a kind of love that is difficult for human beings to have. It is something we can learn from.

Magic Touch

Susanna Sonnenberg

How well you know your own two hands, how they sew, stir, snap; how they grab, pry out knots, press piano keys. You have studied the topography of your knuckles, the finger pads roughed by garden dirt. Your hands tell the story of your life.

Your friend's hand in yours, you dab her nails with polish, hold her fingers steady. You remember when you met, the kickball-game high five, the spark of kinship.

Seventh grade, and you sit beside your crush in the movie theater. His hand is clumsy on the armrest, and he lets his fingers slip over, dangle to reach your hand in your lap. He strokes a centimeter of tender skin inside your palm, over and over, with his fingertip. You stay like that until the movie ends, dazed by first arousal.

Your lover's hand is on your belly, and you lift it to your mouth because he likes it when you do. Your fingers are laced with his everywhere you go, even in summer when you're both sweating, because you don't want to undo from each other.

You clutch your toddler's hand to keep her close in the store. When she was just hours old, her fingers curled like tiny feathers around your thumb. In the numberless repetitions of daily care, you've held her hand to know her—by her pulse, her squirm, and the primal rightness of your fit.

You have your hand on your father's as he dies. Your expert, industrious hand, a woman's, now still, just holding, being strong. You remember: You are five, and your father's hand gloves yours as you cross a busy street on a winter morning. Your hand disappears in his, and you, all trust, prize your own smallness as he warms you and guides you forward, onward.

In Her Shoes

Edwidge Danticat

Becoming a parent's caregiver is a lot like becoming a parent. No one hands you a manual, just a life to love and protect in new, uncharted ways. Except with parents, you have to negotiate that very sensitive space between being helpful and making them feel helpless—between your humility and their humiliation.

One of the things I do to "look after" my mother and myself during her doctors' appointments is take cell phone pictures of her feet—in sandals, in socks, barefoot. I take pictures of her feet with my own feet while lying in bed next to her, with doctors' feet, with lab technicians' feet. I do this sometimes to keep my head down so she can't see my tears as the nurses draw her blood for the thousandth time or as she is being slid through another diagnostic machine that looks like a coffin. But I also take these pictures to remind myself what it's like not just to be my mother's caregiver, but to be my mother.

There's a Haitian Creole expression, *pye poudre*, which is used to talk about people who have traveled long and far. My mother's feet have walked the circumference of my entire world, from Haiti, where we were born, to the United States, where she came when I was four, leaving my brother and me in the care of relatives until she could support us and until U.S. immigration officials finally cleared our reunion, when I was twelve. I used to count my age in Mommy years, subtracting the eight she and I spent apart. In early adulthood, I was the one who was *pye poudre*, venturing away from my mother: going to graduate school, falling in love, having babies of my own. These days, though, my mother and I find ourselves constantly side by side, our four feet lined up, as if waiting to head out on yet another trip, this time together.

A Bolt from the Blue

Julia Alvarez

I was in the tiny bathroom in the back of a plane when I felt the slamming jolt, then the horrible swerve that threw me against the door. Oh Lord, I thought, this is it! Somehow I managed to unbolt the door and scramble out. The flight attendants, already strapped in, waved wildly for me to sit down. As I lunged ahead toward my seat, passengers looked up at me with the stricken expression of creatures who know they are about to die.

"I think we got hit by lightning," said the girl in the seat next to mine. She was from a small town in East Texas, and this was only her second time on an airplane. She had won a trip to England by competing in a high school geography bee and was supposed to make a connecting flight when we landed in Newark.

In the next seat, at the window, sat a young businessman who had been confidently working. Now he looked worried—something that really worries me: when confident-looking businessmen look worried. The laptop was put away. "Something's not right," he said.

The pilot's voice came over the speaker. I heard vaguely through my fear, "Engine number two . . . hit . . . emergency landing . . . New Orleans." When he was done, the voice of a flight attendant came on, reminding us of the emergency procedures she had reviewed before take-off. Of course I never paid attention to this drill, always figuring that if we ever got to the point where we needed to use life jackets, I would have already died of terror.

Now we began a roller-coaster ride through the thunder-clouds. I was ready to faint, but when I saw the face of the girl next to me, I pulled myself together. I reached for her hand and reassured her that we were going to make it. "What a story you're going to tell when you get home!" I said. "After this, London's going to seem like small potatoes."

"Yes, ma'am," she mumbled.

I wondered where I was getting my strength. Then I saw that my other hand was tightly held by a ringed hand. Someone was comforting me—a glamorous young woman across the aisle, the female equivalent of the confident businessman. She must have seen how scared I was and reached over.

"I tell you," she confided, "the problems I brought up on this plane with me sure don't seem real big right now." I loved her Southern drawl, her indiscriminate use of perfume, her soulful squeezes. I was sure that even if I survived a plane crash, I'd have a couple of broken fingers from all the TLC. "Are you okay?" she kept asking me.

Among the many feelings going through my head during those excruciating twenty minutes was pride—pride in how well everybody on board was behaving. No one panicked. No one screamed. As we jolted and screeched our way downward, I could hear small pockets of soothing conversation everywhere.

I thought of something I had heard a friend say about the wonderful gift his dying father had given to the family: He had died peacefully, as if not to alarm any of them about an experience they would all have to go through someday.

And then—yes!—we landed safely. Outside on the ground, attendants and officials were waiting to transfer us to alternate flights. But we passengers clung together. We chatted about the lives we now felt blessed to be living, as difficult or rocky as they might be. The young businessman lamented that he had not had a chance to buy his two little girls presents. An older woman offered him her box of expensive Lindt chocolates, still untouched, tied with a lovely bow. "I shouldn't be eating them anyhow," she said. My glamorous aisle mate took out her cell phone and passed it around to anyone who wanted to make a call to hear the reassuring voice of a loved one.

There was someone I wanted to call. Back in Vermont, my husband, Bill, was anticipating my arrival late that night. He had been complaining that he wasn't getting to see very much of me because of my book tour. That's why I had decided to take this particular flight—oh, yes, one of those stories! I had planned to surprise him by getting in a few hours early. Now I just wanted him to know I was okay and on my way.

When my name was finally called to board my new fight, I felt almost tearful to be parting from people whose lives had so intensely, if briefly, touched mine.

Even now, back on terra firma, walking down a Vermont road, I sometimes hear an airplane and look up at that small, glinting piece of metal. I remember the passengers on that fateful, lucky flight, and I wish I could thank them for the many acts of kindness I witnessed and received. I am indebted to my fellow passengers and wish I could pay them back.

But then, remembering my aisle mate's hand clutching mine while I clutched the hand of the high school student, I feel struck by lightning all over again: The point is not to pay back kindness, but to pass it on.

Whiskered Away

Alexandra Harney

When we found him, he was blind and soaking, slumped in an alleyway, clearly close to death. He struggled to stand, then listed to one side and collapsed again. We watched him for a moment, horrified. And then, because we couldn't just leave him there to die, we picked him up and brought him inside.

We laid him gently on the white expanse of our kitchen counter. After the blurry dark of the monsoon outside, the kitchen felt as bright and quiet as an operating theater. My fiancé, Colin, placed him inside a robin's-egg-blue Tiffany box. We called him Tiffany, and then later, Mr. Tiffany—but most often, we called him Mr. T. That night, while I lay in our bedroom, hiding from the creature's inevitable death, Colin nursed him once an hour with eyedroppers of milk and energy drinks.

He was a street rat, no more than a few days old. His life had begun in the grimy alley beside our apartment in Hong Kong, and to most people, he would have embodied filth and disease. But we saw instead a fragile, unknowable life, and in the three years that followed, we came to see him as no average soul.

Mr. T entered our world during a time of transition. Our wedding was three months away, and I was working seven days a week, often long into the night. My job as a foreign correspondent kept me in constant motion and took me around the world; even owning furniture seemed like a big commitment. I tried not to think about what that would mean for the future. Colin and I planned to have children someday, though some nights we could barely find time to have dinner. Taking in a half-dead rat that needed sustained attention just to survive hadn't been on my agenda.

Which was why, when Colin and I found that Mr. T was miraculously still breathing the next morning, we vowed to set the rat free as soon as he'd recovered fully. He had survived, but he was a wild animal who deserved to live among his own kind. Not to mention that we had both read up on the extensive roster of virulent diseases rodents carry. Unwilling to get attached, I avoided him like, well, the plague.

Still, as he gained strength over the following weeks, we couldn't help celebrating Mr. T's tiny milestones: the moment a week after we found him when he opened his eyes in Colin's palm, the night he lost his fear of our shiny floor tiles, the day he turned a bicycle into a jungle gym, his little black shrimp's eyes flashing in excitement as he clambered over its pedals and wheels.

Mr. T began to make himself at home, confiscating mail, pens, and whole pizza slices and dragging them under the sofa, then chewing a crawl space inside the sofa itself. It was clear he intended to settle in for the long haul. But could we really keep this animal? On the other hand, was it even feasible for Mr. T to reenter the wild? We called a professor at Oxford University who specialized in rat behavior. He told us that domesticated rats set free in the forest begin acting like wild rats within a few hours. There was nothing stopping us from bidding Mr. T adieu and moving on with our lives.

Nothing except the fact that we couldn't resist his charms. Already, he'd begun to train us in his care. By

knocking over his dinner dishes or leaving them untouched, he made it clear that most vegetables—carrots,
green beans, peppers—were inedible unless drenched in
butter. He would eat peas, but only when shelled; the tops,
but never the stalks, of broccoli; blueberries, but only if
cut in half. His favorite foods were mushroom pâté, sushi,
and scrambled eggs. A few drops of beer were always ap-
preciated. We prepared him two hot meals a day, which he
ate with surgical precision, extracting the fattiest morsels
first. He was too cute to let go.

Colin built Mr. T a five-story dwelling from wood and
chicken wire, which we furnished with the cushions of the
sofa he had destroyed. Mr. T compulsively redesigned his
home, shredding the cushions and shoving bits of stuffing
into the gaps in the chicken wire. Sometimes he would
snuggle under my palm, pushing his nose into the V
between my thumb and forefinger. If I tried to move away,
he would grip my fingers with powder-pink, gummy-palmed
paws.

I began to see Hong Kong as a place teeming with more
than just human life: the giant hoary moth wrapped around
the corner of an office building; the bird squatting on the
pavement outside a watch shop; the feral dogs that patrolled

the area behind our apartment building. One afternoon, after noticing one of Mr. T's grubbier cousins in the same alley where we had found him, I realized that the line we draw between animals that are socially acceptable and those we find repugnant can be awfully arbitrary.

As Mr. T steadily pawed his way into our hearts, Colin and I identified, for the first time in our lives, as parents. My husband was a rational and generous father, and I was a neurotic, fussy mom. Colin tried to see the world through Mr. T's eyes, adding a solid wooden door to Mr. T's home when he realized how much he liked his privacy, or adhesive sandpaper when he saw Mr. T slip on his ramps. Meanwhile, I obsessed over Mr. T's health, fearing that every nap or failed attempt to mount the coffee table signaled terminal illness.

I felt our world conforming to Mr. T's needs—and I loved it. Colin and I stopped going out to dinner as often and instead spent evenings in our living room, beaming proudly as Mr. T dragged apples and socks into his house with great seriousness. Some nights, we stayed up on the sofa until two, three, four in the morning, waiting for the nocturnal Mr. T to rouse himself and pad downstairs. We stopped traveling together so one of us could always be home to keep him company, and when that was impossible, we enlisted house sitters and left an instruction manual nearly an inch thick. At parties we matched our friends' tales of their children with news of Mr. T's latest tricks, his most recent fascinations: wooden knives and forks, starchy restaurant napkins, salmon sashimi. I posted photos on Facebook of Mr. T eating green beans, his tiny paws covered in tomato sauce, or Mr. T in repose, his whiskers a halo around his face.

And all the while, we grappled with the fact that Mr. T didn't have much time. On the streets, most rats die before their first birthday. In captivity, many die by three. Not long after he turned two, Mr. T's once rapid pace slowed to a jog, then a waddle, and he began to sleep more solidly through the days. But he was determined to keep going. When, as I had often worried he might, he developed a tumor—it was as large as his head—we found a microsurgeon who removed it, and Mr. T sprinted across our living room the same day. When a spinal condition paralyzed his back legs, he adapted by pulling himself up and down the ramps with his front paws.

One night he began to struggle to breathe. This time the surgeon couldn't save him. Mr. T died in Colin's hands.

We had him cremated and held a small ceremony in which we scattered some of his ashes in the park behind our apartment building so he could rest near his family. We put the remainder of his ashes in an urn, which we placed beside a picture of him in our living room, and tried to adjust to the sad fact that we didn't get to be Mr. T's mom and dad anymore. But shortly after his passing, Colin and I became parents to a son, whom we named Louis T.

A few years earlier, we had struggled to find even a spare hour in the day—but Mr. T taught us how to make room in our lives for the future we wanted, to be more empathetic, more patient. He taught us to love unconditionally. We'd found Mr. T in one of life's interstices, between dating and marriage, coupledom and parenthood. If it had been a dog or a cat slumped in our alleyway that night, there would be no story to tell. We would have brought the animal to a shelter. Knowing that nobody would do that for Mr. T made us bring him into our home, and doing so made all the difference.

Some of our friends and family just didn't get Mr. T. They never understood how we could love a rat. We never understood how, if you had the pleasure of meeting him, it was possible not to.

To the End

Christy K. Mack

One sunny summer day six years ago, my friend Susan turned to me and said, "Christy, you're going to take me there." She'd just been told she had leukemia, and she and her daughter had come to my house to talk. Sitting in my garden, the three of us shared our thoughts about life and death and God. I didn't know what she meant by "take me there," and for some reason, I didn't ask. I simply let the words hang in the air.

We had been friends for twenty years. We shared the same birthday. Her children, Sara and Geoff, grew up with mine. Along the way, Susan battled a series of major illnesses: two breast cancers, a tumor in her spinal cord, uterine cancer, lymphatic cancer. But until leukemia took her life at the age of fifty-three, she refused to give up. She confided to me her fear of suffering and death, yet she was strong, dignified, and graceful, never letting anyone sense the devastation that was taking over her body and her life.

A month after that beautiful day at my house, Sara called me from the intensive care unit: Her mother wasn't expected to make it through the evening. I arrived at the hospital around five thirty on a dreary, rainy afternoon. I prayed that I would be whatever Susan needed me to be. My heart ached. My stomach was in knots. I was afraid I would fail her. I didn't know what to expect or what I was supposed to do.

Her room was filled with machines, IV drips, and monitors. The lights were dimmed, the curtains drawn, the door shut. Everything was eerily quiet. Susan's liver had shut down, and her blood pressure was dangerously low. All we could do was hold her hand, arrange her pillows to keep her comfortable, watch the drips and monitors, and pray.

For hours that was our vigil as Susan slipped in and out of awareness. She'd grow restless. Her blood pressure would fall to new lows. Then she'd fight, and her blood pressure would shoot up, only to plummet as she eased back onto the pillows. For hours she continued to draw on every bit of strength she had, and with each effort, she grew weaker. She was fighting a losing battle. She was exhausted, and her worst fears were being realized—she was suffering, in enormous pain. We felt helpless. Watching her was unbearable, and we knew that she could not go on.

And then, as though she realized it, too, Susan became very still. She slowly turned her face toward me and locked her eyes with mine, and though she didn't say a word, I heard her voice clearly: "Christy, take me there."

Suddenly I understood what she had meant sitting in my garden. She had known that when the time came, she would not be able to let go, that no matter what, she was going to struggle to live. She could not believe it would be okay to leave this earth or her children. And, knowing she'd be unable to make the journey alone, she had wanted me to help.

It was twelve fifteen in the morning. I gathered my strength and asked Sara if she had told her mother that it was okay to let go. She answered with heartbreaking sadness, "Yes, many times."

I said, "Well, Sara, with your permission, I'd like to start talking to your mom."

And so Susan and I began our journey.

For the next two and a half hours, I sat inches away from her, our eyes locked as if we were looking into each other's souls. I told her it was time to let go, that it was okay to let go. I told her I had taken her hand and we were going to set off on a trip down a road together, just like all the other roads we had traveled, except that this would be the most glorious trip of all. I explained that I could go only so far with her, and that when the time came, her mother would be waiting to take her hand and walk with her the rest of the way.

I didn't know if she could hear any of the words I was saying, but after a while, I sensed a change in her, a calming. I didn't dare look at the monitors to see if she was beginning to surrender; I was afraid to lose the connection between us.

I don't know how I knew what to say, but the words kept coming. I told her that she had completed her path and had done everything God had asked her to do and more. Her children loved her. I loved her. I assured her that she was not alone—that pieces of us were going with her. I repeated that she had worked her whole life for this moment and now she was ready to walk with me, hand in hand, to greet her mother and live in the most glorious of all realms with her God. She had earned her place in the heaven she envisioned, a place of everlasting peace and unconditional love. I kept telling her that it was time. Her journey on this earth was over.

My one-sided conversation continued as we held hands. And then, before I could understand what was happening, the room began to change. The walls, IV drips, machines, and monitors, even the bed Susan was in, slowly disappeared as she and I became immersed in a pool of golden light. Bathed in the light, in silence, we gazed even more deeply into each other's eyes. I had never experienced anything like it, and yet it seemed perfectly natural. I was awed by the beauty of the moment and the utter serenity of the light; I was comforted by the spiritual connection. Susan had let me in to see what she was experiencing, and I was moved with unspeakable gratitude. She was telling me she was nearing the end, so I told her that I was giving her hand a loving squeeze and placing it carefully in her mother's hand, that I knew she could see her mother, and that it was time to go the rest of the way with her. I told her to focus on how good it felt to feel her mother's hand in hers again, to feel the softness of her touch, the warmth of her embrace.

That's when Susan finally, slowly, turned away from me. She focused on something straight ahead, as if looking in the direction of her journey.

For a long few seconds, she stopped breathing. The tension in her face was replaced by softness—the softness that comes with acceptance. Turning her gaze from mine, I understood, was her way of encouraging me; she knew that these last moments would be very difficult for me. So when she stopped breathing, I stopped talking and simply caressed her cheek and smoothed her hair. I was waiting for the pulse in her neck that I knew would come, signaling another fight to live. When the beat came, she took a single big breath. I reassured her that it was okay. She could go. She was almost there. I waited for the next beat and the next breath, and the next, and the next, reassuring her that all was as it should be. Time stopped. She was still. Our little corner of the world waited. Stroking her cheek, I whispered, "You're right there, Susan, I know it. Cross the threshold, my special friend." And she did. In peace.

Sara and I reached across the bed, clutched each other's hands atop her mother's lap, squeezed hard, and cried.

Susan blessed me with her love, taught me with her spirit, and honored me with her final wish. What she and I shared the night she died was a precious gift of friendship, emotionally profound and sacred in its perfection. It broke my heart. It strengthened my soul.

Somewhere Safe

Run my dear,
from anything
that may not strengthen
your precious budding wings.

—HAFIZ

Homes of the Brave

Rachel Starnes

The light here, in this serene home I've made, is stuck at sunny midmorning. It's always a weekend, always summer. Every room is one my husband could've just left to go grab a cup of coffee, and soon he'll be back to enjoy it with me before our boys come thundering in.

Except there is no midmorning light, no endless summer. I'm exhausted, huddled before my laptop in a temporary home in a temporary town, my toddlers finally in bed, four loads of laundry waiting. I'm scrolling through images I've gathered, which add up, detail by detail, to my Forever Home, where I fantasize about us living when Ross is no longer an active-duty navy pilot.

I'm one of many military spouses curating such a home

on Pinterest, a vision of the future to hold on to when the present is hard to bear. My husband's absence is a reality I've grown used to during his twelve years in the navy. This time it's only a month. Sometimes it's eight. For some, it will be forever. Perspective is important.

Maybe it's strange to focus on the kitchen island and claw-foot tub of a house that doesn't exist. Or maybe it's not strange for us wives to converse this way, pinning and repinning images, when there are so many things we *can't* say—that we update wills with disturbing frequency, that we're tired of repacking every eight months and watching the one we love leave.

This is the house we can paint, where we can make plans that aren't subverted by a last-minute change in orders. This is where Dad returns every night, where duffel bags aren't packed and waiting by the door. These boards give us more than ideas about where we might want to live. They let us dream, for a moment, of finally coming home.

At My Fingertips

Kaui Hart Hemmings

Sometimes the way I get through my day is by reminding myself that it will end. That period when I couldn't sell my novel? It came to an end. Those months of bewilderment with a colicky baby? The baby, now ten, stopped crying a long time ago. Things change. Nothing lasts forever. The sun rises, the sun sets. It's an inevitable, often lovely cycle.

My husband and I have a four-year-old whom we adopted from Ethiopia when he was ten months old. He's happy, full of energy, curious, loving. He's also aggressive, impulsive, hyperactive. He's been kicked out of three preschools in a year. The previous one endured him for seven days. His last one just gave him the heave-ho after two weeks. Attention-deficit/hyperactivity disorder, oppositional defiant disorder, attachment disorder, sensory integration disorder, autism, Asperger's. It could be any of the above or none of them—a mere delay, an "unreadiness" for school, teachers who turned their backs too soon. We don't know.

At first my husband and I corrected, rewarded, took away, enforced, raised our voices, asked him why. After the second school we went to play therapy, to parenting classes. We took advice from friends, family, strangers.

The treasure we found in this pile was so obvious, but it took us far too long to see it. It was the power of praise—for using a nice voice, for trying to solve a problem, for being calm and kind. We've changed the way we speak to our son. We say things like "I like how sweet your voice sounds" and "I love playing with you." Sometimes it sounds as though we've been replaced by Mister Rogers; sometimes we have to go outside for a sarcasm break. But in the midst of this heartache, of seeing our child rejected again and again, praise and kindness and love are the only things we've got.

Of course, it's hard to praise him when you get a phone call saying you have to pick up your child because he cried, fought, wouldn't stop saying "stupid." Months ago I went to get him from school, and after I put him in the car, I couldn't stop crying. I hid it as best I could, trying to think of what to do. Praise? I couldn't praise just then. I thought back to that moment when we saw just how simple the answer was, and I thought: What's logical? What's obvious? What's at my fingertips? I live in Hawaii. The ocean. I didn't care that the beach would feel like a reward. I decided not to take that away from either of us. I drove there, silent. We got out, silent. I took off his shirt and stripped down to my bathing suit. I walked him into the ocean, and then I went underwater and cried. I broke the surface and looked at my son, happily splashing in the surf, a confident, strong swimmer.

What was obvious is that we had the mountain range behind us and the ocean before us. What's obvious is that we will change. What's obvious is that the sun will set and rise and that everything can be attempted again.

Nice Talking to You

Sophie McManus

As a twentysomething, I measured life by the hour, waiting tables. It was fun, sneaking bottles of champagne to the line cooks in exchange for an end-of-shift steak. Fun, too, the nights on Brooklyn rooftops under the jagged constellation of city lights, chain-smoking and making clever talk. Love and purpose—those supposed joys—were for someone else, in some other kind of life. I'd had no luck with them. But then one day I ran into a friend I hadn't seen in a while. She paused, searching for what she knew of me.

"How's your cat?" she asked.

She was the fourth person in a row who couldn't think of anything else.

"Great," I said, and burst into tears.

I spent my initial therapy sessions hiding in plain sight by making my psychotherapist, Janet, laugh, and privately inspecting the knickknacks on her shelves and speculating as to why the one personal fact she'd shared with me was her love of string cheese.

But slowly, despite myself, the habit of self-reflection replaced the habit of avoidance. With Janet, I was rehearsing being vulnerable around, connected to, another human being. Her express mission was to help me, to be kind, and to expect nothing in return. And so I learned to expect kindness.

Actively considering your past puts you in the habit of considering the present. I wanted to be a writer. Was I writing? Janet asked. Had I applied to the graduate program I'd mentioned? It's hard to forget your hopes when someone is minding them. And so I became the person doing the minding.

I left therapy and New York City for a writing fellowship by the sea. The session before our last, Janet said, "You have a homework assignment."

Seven years, and she'd never made a request.

"What is it?" I asked.

"You'll figure it out."

During the fellowship, I would write a book. I would meet my future husband. I would find the work that gives my life meaning. And I would know that it was therapy that allowed all this, that let me believe such marvels could be waiting for me.

But before that, as my last hour with Janet was ending, I screwed up my courage. "Thank you for helping me," I said, my voice unsteady.

Gratitude. My homework had been to admit that I'd needed her and that no harm had come of that need. To admit, in even this limited way, love.

The Gang's All Here

Leesa Suzman

I wasn't raised to be high maintenance. My mother's idea of special-occasion makeup is rubbing a little lipstick on her cheeks, and she has never had a facial, manicure, pedicure, or massage because she deems them frivolous. Up until the summer of my twenty-fifth birthday, my most self-indulgent weekly ritual was pouring a little baby oil into my Sunday-night bath. But every Friday evening for the past seven years, I've had a standing appointment at La Petite, a tiny, nondescript storefront nail salon on Manhattan's Upper East Side, where I go for weekly manicures, biweekly pedicures, a monthly waxing, and an array of spa services that leave me feeling as well-groomed as a Palm Beach socialite.

I often arrive at La Petite straight from the office, still reeling from whatever rush-hour jam has made me five minutes late—and I'm continually amazed at how, in a city where calm places are as scarce as cheap apartments, my pulse immediately slows at the door. I'm a sucker for the hand-painted rendering of Versailles covering an entire wall (commissioned by Hanna, La Petite's thirty-something Polish owner), the baskets overflowing with snacks brought by customers, the black Ikea lounge chairs where you can linger long after your toe polish has dried, and the sometimes spirited, sometimes melancholy, conversations among the regulars—women who have revealed secrets to me that have caused my jaw to drop or my heart to ache but whose last names I'll probably never know.

My weekly pilgrimages to La Petite began after a brutal breakup. That summer I would often take long walks around my neighborhood, ostensibly for the exercise or on an errand but really hoping I'd run into someone to connect with. On one of those walks, I turned a corner onto a side street and found La Petite. I don't remember what first drew me in, other than the promise of air-conditioning on a sweltering day, but I know why I sat there for almost an hour waiting for the next available manicure appointment:

the laughter that spilled out the door as I entered. The mood inside was upbeat, even joyous, and there seemed to be no distinction between customers and employees—everybody was in the thick of the conversation. This was clearly not your average assembly-line New York City nail shop, where the only exchanges between the polishers and the polished usually revolve around the question "What color?" Nor was it the kind of designer spa you often find on the Upper East Side, where securing an appointment with a star manicurist can be a nail-biting experience.

La Petite quickly became my Cheers—a place I return to again and again, where everybody does indeed know my name. There are the obvious beauty benefits: I love having hands that always look groomed and legs that always feel smooth. But I don't crave the beauty treatments half as much as the familiar faces, the Friday-night routine, and the Norm-style greeting that I still receive when I enter.

There's always common ground to cover, everything from neighborhood news to the deep stuff. Need a new apartment? Somebody always has a suggestion. A wedding dress? Have you been to . . . ? A new boyfriend? Let me tell you about my friend Jed.

The faces have changed somewhat over the years, but

the communal, reunion-like spirit of Friday nights at La Petite endures. These women have seen me through new jobs, new loves, eventually true love, a new last name, and most recently the various stages of pending motherhood. In fact, La Petite was the first place I brought my newborn daughter. I was intent on introducing her to Hanna and the gang and on placing her picture on a mirrored pillar covered with dozens of snapshots of customers' children. Weeks earlier Hanna had painted a question mark in red nail polish on the pillar. It was her way of letting me know she was saving a space on the La Petite family tree.

Planes, Trains, and Automobiles

Katie Arnold-Ratliff

— ❧ —

Next time you find yourself stuck on the road
Maddened by gridlock, horrifically slowed,
Decide it's a chance (increasingly rare)
To sit for a while and placidly stare
At scenery scrolling, a blur of a view,
The fine fellow travelers in cars around you—
And wonder, *Who are they? And what do they do?*

It's stressful to sit when you're running behind,
As predicaments go, it's among the least kind.
But if your confinement cannot be avoided,
Consider this fact: It *can* be exploited.
Yes, stalls are dulling, but let us convey:

The boring get bored; the rest find their way—
To reverie, fantasy, a mental soiree.

Your mind is a marvel, a captive's best friend!
It can wander and ponder and scheme to no end.
Use immobile moments to make lists, enact plays,
Compose epic poems, sing French cabaret.
In the car that you pilot, this space all your own,
You're free to make merry wherever you roam.
So when you are forced to park in your lane,
Enjoy the advantage of being detained.
Surrender to stillness, feel free—and stay sane.

Mysterious Ways

I felt myself trembling on the brink of a fabulous
discovery, as though any morning it was all going
to come together—my future, my past, the whole of my
life—and I was going to sit up in bed like a
thunderbolt and say *oh! oh! oh!*

—DONNA TARTT, *THE SECRET HISTORY*

Bed, Bath, and the Great Beyond

Alex Banner

Before my dad died, he wanted two things: for me to get into jazz, and to own a Tingler, one of those spidery head-scratcher things. After he got sick, the head scratcher fell down the priority list, but jazz—that was important. One day just before he went into the hospital for the last time, he and I drove around listening to music. He played me a track by Les McCann and Eddie Harris—a live performance of "Cold Duck Time." It had a good groove. He gave me three CDs, each with a different version of that song.

When my dad was near the end, his best friend, my brother, and I sat with him while he played us the Mahalia Jackson and Duke Ellington record *Black, Brown and*

Beige. It was a profound thing—us men, together, listening in silence to this woman's voice. We knew we were saying good-bye. The last song we heard was "Come Sunday," and I remember thinking, This is the most beautiful song there ever was.

He died on a Wednesday, ten years ago last October. Not long after, my mom called, crying and laughing at the same time. She had just come from Bed Bath & Beyond, where she found a Tingler in a discount bin. She thought she owed it to my dad to buy it and took it to the counter. The clerk told her Bed Bath & Beyond didn't carry Tinglers. She could just have it, he said. My mom didn't call it a sign, but it was *something*, she said, something from beyond—or the beyond part of Bed Bath & Beyond, at least. She felt like he had visited her.

And then he came to visit me. I was working as a mason at the time, spending my days digging holes. One day, I was four feet into the ground, listening to Chucho Valdés's version of "Cold Duck Time" on my headphones, when I hit something: a little white dove carved out of stone. I cried into the hole I'd dug.

Two months later, I got laid off. For weeks I walked around San Francisco, asking for work at every job site I saw. I must have left a hundred résumés. One day I was so beat up, so broke and broken, I put on "Come Sunday" to feel better. I hadn't heard it since that day with my dad. And as it played, I got a call from a guy offering me an apprenticeship as a woodworker. I had no experience, but something told me to say yes.

I'd never believed in an afterlife, in heaven and hell. I'm not sure just what I believe now. But I do know that when people die, they don't just die.

I still think "Come Sunday" is the most beautiful song ever recorded, though I don't listen to it much. I prefer to save it. I keep the dove on a high shelf, watching over my house. I own my own woodworking business. And I use the Tingler a lot. It feels so good—like a gentle hand, reaching out to touch.

The Doubter's Dilemma

Kelly Corrigan

My mother is fond of telling me I'm overthinking it—"it" being anything from the virtues of organic mulch for my flower beds to which booster seats to buy for my daughters— so you can imagine how she feels about my religious ambivalence. While it's not quite true to say she was thirty with three kids before she met someone who wasn't Catholic, it's close enough. Perhaps as a consequence, she is not a woman who has frittered away her days critiquing her religion. Instead she prays, mostly for her children, who she so hoped would inherit her bulletproof faith but who are more likely to drive away with her navy-blue Buick and a leftover case of Chardonnay she bought at a discount in Delaware. Both my parents shudder over our discerning, noncommittal generation that has something to say about everything but nowhere to go on Sunday mornings.

I envy my parents' faith. Supplication, I've often thought, must be easier on the body than Tums and Ambien. And how contenting it must be to believe that someday everyone you love will be in one place and will stay there forever. Who wouldn't want that destiny? But for all its comforting appeal, I rarely go to church and have read only a few chapters of the Bible. Even when disaster struck my family hard, I did not fall to my knees and petition the God of my childhood.

In autumn 2004, both my father and I were diagnosed with late-stage cancer. I was thirty-six, and the seven-centimeter tumor behind my nipple was technically my second cancer. (In my mid-twenties, I'd had a melanoma as big as a pencil eraser removed from my calf, leaving a little divot and a long scar that reminds me to use sunblock and stay in the shade at midday.) My dad was seventy-four, and the scattered tumors around his bladder marked round three for him.

The day my doctor called with the diagnosis, I hung up the phone, looked over the heads of my kids, and mouthed to my husband, "It's cancer." Then, after a long hug, a cold Corona, and a cigarette (I had squirreled away a half-smoked pack after a party the year before, and for reasons I can't explain, I couldn't wait to suck down a Merit Ultra Light that afternoon), we went to the computer and started searching for information on "invasive ductal carcinoma." My father got his diagnosis in person; after thanking the doctor and scheduling a slew of tests, he and my mother slid into the Buick and drove down to St. Colman's, their favorite little church, for noon Mass. They gave it to God; we gave it to Google.

Over the course of a year, my dad and I both got better, and, especially in his case, people said it was miraculous. At the very least, it was unexpected. Perhaps even unexplainable, though not to Mom, who summed it up in one word: *prayer.* "People around the world were praying for your father," she explained ("around the world" referring primarily to a high school friend of mine who lived in Moscow and had always been fond of my dad).

I had both always prayed and never prayed, which is to say that I often found myself in bed at the end of a day saying to no one in particular, "Thank you for this good man beside me and those girls in the other room." But I had not beseeched God to make me well, had not begged God for my father's life. Among other things, I didn't want to be—to borrow from sixth-grade parlance—a *user*, a phony who thought she could get what she wanted by conveniently nuzzling up to someone she usually snubbed.

After my dad recovered, I talked to an old friend about my parents' confidence in prayer and their belief that God had intervened. Rather than praise the inexplicable glory of God, my friend thought we should exalt the devotion and ingenuity of man. Or, as she put it: "It just bugs me how people want to give all the credit away, as if we were all just useless sinners who didn't know how to take care of ourselves or each other." In other words, maybe it wasn't prayer that made my dad better—maybe it was all that chemo. Or the scope with tiny scissors that removed nine moldy tumors from his bladder without his even having to check in to the OR. Or the meticulous doctor who managed his case with such vigilance.

I liked my friend's take on things: Up with people and their hard work and cool inventions. But I kept thinking back to my father's initial prognosis. The urologist to whom I attributed my dad's stunning recovery had told us to brace for the worst. Ten months later, when he declared my father a healthy man, that same doctor said he couldn't explain "how on earth" my dad was disease-free. Could I really give all the credit to a doctor who shrugged his shoulders and said it was anybody's guess how George Corrigan survived?

The art of growing up is coming to terms with the disturbing fact that even the very smartest people don't always have the answers. Let us remember that it was only a generation or so ago when new mothers smoked cigarettes on the maternity ward while nurses fed the infants nice big bottles of formula. Only a few years ago, children were still being taught to believe that poor Pluto was a planet. If history teaches us anything, it's that the truth is subject to change. This means that what is standard practice now may someday be eschewed, in the same way that no health-conscious person puts plastic in the microwave anymore. It also means that notions we now consider dubious may, somewhere down the road, become widely accepted. So might we eventually say, "Can you believe that people used to doubt the power of prayer?"

In fact, the federal government has underwritten elaborate studies asking this very question. Online, I've found a pile of research suggesting a measurable, therapeutic benefit to prayer and prayerful meditation. Sure, the link can be explained away; like any type of quiet meditation, prayer is relaxing, and relaxation has proven physiological benefits. But a click away from the reports was a survey of physicians—a clear majority of whom pray for their patients. So prayer isn't just for my gullible parents. And if doctors can get to belief, might I?

If there is a God, he knows how much I want there to be more to human existence than a series of discrete physical experiences that start with birth and end with death. I want all of us—and all our lives—to be meaningful. But small. I'd be elated to learn that this go-round is only part one of something that has a thousand parts. I'd love to laugh at this life from a distance. As it is, I relish the fact that I am one of six billion people the way my mother revels in Pavarotti's recording of the "Ave Maria." Being one in six billion means my life can't possibly matter to anyone but me and my little flock—which means that all my mistakes and failures and anxieties are utterly inconsequential. When I forget this, when things begin to matter too much and I find it hard to get a good, deep breath, I close my eyes and imagine flying over houses, lifting off the roofs, and seeing all the people whose existence is concurrent with mine. I imagine them arguing, cooking, hugging, suffering and laughing, living and dying. Each of us a little bitty fish in an inconceivably large pond, swimming in circles, nothing to do but enjoy the water.

But maybe that's an incomplete picture. Maybe there's something between and around and inside all six billion of us, and maybe that something knows every hair on each of our heads. Maybe we are not anonymous. Wouldn't that be outrageous? And beautiful?

Faith is the tallest order, the toughest nut: the humbling of yourself before purposes you don't—and cannot ever—comprehend. Let's face it, believing that there is a God who might get involved in your tiny little life is beyond anti-intellectual. And this is why I doubt. But when I'm honest with myself, I have to admit that there's doubt within my doubt. And every time I remind myself of that, I think of Voltaire's confounding line: "Doubt is not a pleasant condition, but certainty is an absurd one." So I let my parents share their faith with our children. When we visit Philadelphia, where my parents live, I let them take our daughters to church. At night, my mom gets the girls on their knees and shows them how to cross themselves and position their hands and bow their heads. It is a lovely sight, and I would never discourage it. Of course, when we get back home to California, the girls are loaded with new ideas and questions they're counting on me to answer.

Claire, who is a senior in preschool, recently asked what lights are made of. After I told her something about electricity and filaments and Thomas Edison, she said, "In church, they said Jesus is a light." Georgia, a first grader, reprimanded me for saying "Oh my God." "*God* is a bad word," she said. To which I heard myself say, "Oh no, honey. *God* is not a bad word. *God* is a very good word." Both girls have asked if they could be the Holy Ghost for Halloween.

Regardless of where I am on the spectrum from atheism to theism, I'd rather my girls be grounded in something, even something that seems too good or crazy to be true. This is why, when the girls ask me about God, I say that people believe all kinds of things and no one really knows, including me, but that I *hope.* Then I tell them what my husband, with tears in his eyes, recently told me: I say being with them is the most spiritual experience of my life—the highest high, the deepest yes, the most staggering gift—and that gift must have come from somewhere.

And what about all the little gifts, the everyday stuff

like a good cantaloupe or a great public school teacher or the rebate check coming just in time? For that, I've taken to saying grace. At the dinner table we all hold hands while I talk about our friends, our family, our health. Then my husband, generally prompted by my raised eyebrow, says a prayer for the people we know who are having trouble. The girls mostly tolerate all this (sometimes adding a thank-you for a Popsicle or a playdate) and look forward to saying "Amen," after which we take turns rising from our seats to do a family wave, as if the home team had just scored.

It feels good, saying grace. But for now, that's as far as I've gotten—just another person pulsing with thankfulness, wondering what will happen next. Someday—despite all medications and all prayers—people in our lives will get sick and will not get better. Georgia and Claire will ask me where they went, and I'll probably be wondering the same thing. Have they gone to a paradise, a separate plane of existence where God holds them in the palm of his hand? Are they internalized in the people who are left behind? Do they become part of the earth and therefore an endless part of the cycle of life?

If you asked my dad, he'd assure you that heaven exists and *boy, are you gonna love it.* Just like if you asked him why I got better, he'd say something about how God wants me to be here. I tell him I got better because of four chemotherapies, each an impressive creation of man. But that just makes him laugh, shake his head, and flash his big, knowing smile. "Aw, lovey," he says, "don't you see? What do you think makes a man spend his days trying to cure cancer?"

Witness Trees

Bob Hicok

Some people, told of witness trees,

pause in chopping a carrot

or loosening a lug nut and ask,

witness to what? So while salad

is made, or getting from A to B

is repaired, these people

listen to the story

of the Burnside Bridge sycamore,

alive at Antietam, bloodiest day

of the war, or the Appomattox Court House

honey locust, just coming to leaf

as Lee surrendered, and say, at the end,

Cool. Then the chopping

continues with its two sounds,

the slight snap to the separation

of carrot from carrot, the harder crack

of knife against cutting board,

or the sigh, also slight, of a lug nut

as it's tightened against a wheel. In time,

these people put their hands

under water and say, not so much to you

but to the window in front of the sink,

Think of all the things

trees have seen. Then it's time

for dinner, or to leave, and a month passes,

or a year, before two fawns

cross in front of the car, or the man

you've just given a dollar to

lifts his shirt to the start

of the 23rd Psalm tattooed

to his chest, "The Lord is my shepherd,

I shall not want," when some people

say, *I feel like one of those trees,*

you know? And you do know.

You make a good salad, change

a wicked tire, you're one of those people,

watching, listening, a witness
to whatever this is,
for as long as it is
amazing, isn't it, that I could call you
right now and say, *They still*
can't talk to dolphins
but are closer, as I still
can't say everything I want to
but am closer, for trying, to God,
if you must, to spirit, if you will,
to what's never easy for people
like us: life, breath, the sheer volume
of wonder.

The Empty Space

Sasha Sagan

Whenever a shift occurs in her life, even if it's something small—a restaurant goes out of business, a teacup shatters—my mother always says the same thing: "There is no refuge from change in the cosmos."

Some changes are quick. Others take a long time to fully reveal themselves. When a star dies, the darkness left by its absence ripples through the universe at the speed of light, which may seem impossibly fast—but over the great distances of space, even that isn't fast enough. The dead stars appear to shine, but they're long gone.

The defining change of my life was the death of my father. I was fourteen. For years I would dream he'd returned with an elaborate explanation for where he'd been, then I'd wake up crushed. The loss of his light—the full impact of his absence—took years to reach me.

Sixteen years after his death from a long illness, I sat in the lobby of a midtown Manhattan hotel with my husband-to-be, our wedding planner, and the lead singer of our wedding band.

"Are you doing a father-daughter dance?" the bandleader asked.

I felt a fresh ripple of grief. "No, my dad passed away," I said.

The singer flinched, then smiled. "Your father will be watching over you on your special day," she said.

The sentiment was kind, but I don't believe in an afterlife. I—like my late father, the astronomer Carl Sagan—believe only in what can be proved. Jon, my fiancé, squeezed my hand. I made a noncommittal sound and changed the subject.

I miss my dad at every birthday and Thanksgiving, every graduation and send-off, every achievement and failure—every day. But there was something about a wedding, about my wedding, that made the longing worse. However antiquated the reason, weddings center on the father-daughter relationship. He walks you down the aisle, leads you in that first dance, gives you away to the man who will love you in his place.

Jon and I grew up together in Ithaca, New York. For many years we were acquaintances, then friends, then lovers. Early in our relationship we went to a friend's wedding, where the bride's father described how much he loved his daughter, how precious their relationship was. I was heartsick. I was jealous. I cried in the ladies' room. When my time came, a wedding without my dad would be too awful to face. Why invite everyone I knew to come stare at the hole in my life? Later that night Jon and I sat in Central Park, and for the first time I let him see the depth of my grief. Jon didn't tell me a happy lie, didn't say everything would be okay. He just held me, tears wetting his own face. My dad wrote a book that contains the line "For small creatures such as we the vastness is bearable only through love." For that and a million other reasons, there was no question about my answer when Jon knelt in the garden of our favorite restaurant and asked me to be his wife.

My father couldn't walk me down the aisle, no matter how much I wanted him to, but I knew I had to somehow feel his presence at our wedding. I decided we should get married somewhere he and I had been together. I didn't believe his spirit would be there, but I knew my memories of him would be.

Then on a trip home to Ithaca, Jon and I visited the Herbert F. Johnson Museum of Art, a modernist structure on the Cornell campus. When I was small, my father would take me there to see a famous Giacometti sculpture and the Japanese scrolls. It was the site of his memorial service in 1996. But that day Jon and I saw something new. On the ceiling of a massive open-air room that juts out from the museum, the artist Leo Villareal had used a framework of thousands of lights to create a constantly morphing, whooshing depiction of deep space. He called the piece *Cosmos*—a tribute to my father's work and to the grandeur of what Dad called "all that is or ever was or ever will be."

That autumn, my mother and grandfather walked me down the aisle on the top floor of the museum, which overlooks our beloved town. After cocktails and speeches, the band played, and Jon and I danced under Villareal's ever-changing tableau, before our friends and family put us in chairs and lifted us skyward. Looking at the beautiful and good man I married, and looking up at the legacy of the beautiful and good man I lost, I was happy in a way I hadn't believed possible. There is no refuge from change in the cosmos, or from the heartbreak those changes can bring. But in the midst of all that is, was, or ever will be, there is a light that keeps shining, reaching us from far away.

A Conversation with Pema Chödrön

Oprah Winfrey

In the early 1970s, Pema Chödrön, born Dierdre Blomfield-Brown, was a married mother of two living in California and working as an elementary school teacher. When she was in her mid-twenties, Pema and her husband divorced. Eight years later, she remarried. One day, Pema's second husband told her he intended to leave her for another woman, and Pema fell into an intense depression. Heartbroken, she struggled to find a way to break through her sadness. By chance, she came across a magazine that was open to an article by Chögyam Trungpa, a renowned Tibetan Buddhist meditation teacher; it described how pain can bring us closer to the truth. The words put Pema

on the trajectory that would change her: less than two years later, she took a Buddhist vow to spend the rest of her life helping others seek enlightenment and end their suffering. Chögyam Trungpa became her teacher, and in 1981, Pema became the first American woman to become a fully ordained Buddhist nun in the Tibetan tradition. She was given the name Pema Chödrön, which means "lotus torch of the dharma" (a loose translation might be "lamp of the truth").

In 2008, Pema and I sat down for a conversation in which she shared her essential belief about the inevitable pain we all experience: that it can create the possibility of a more joyful life.

OPRAH: You were an average mother of two, and then you became a Buddhist nun. What did you read in that article that put you on this path?

PEMA: I became involved in Buddhism in a way that's very appealing to a lot of people because of the fact that their lives fall apart, which is what happened to me. When my second marriage broke up, it just floored me, but I had some kind of fundamental sanity that kept saying, "There's something very profound in this that will teach you something," so I started looking for it. The first line of Chögyam Trungpa's article "Working with Negativity" read, "We all experience negativity—the basic aggression of wanting things to be different than they are." Everything else was saying, "Look at the positive side," and this said, "Stay with your experience." That's how it started.

OPRAH: Is that what you advise we do when things fall apart—stay with it?

PEMA: Yes. The problem is that we have so little tolerance for uncomfortable feelings. I'm not even talking about unpleasant outer circumstances, but that feeling in your stomach of "I don't want this to be happening." You try to escape it in some way, but if somehow you could stay present and touch the rawness of the experience, you can really learn something.

OPRAH: What happens if you choose not to sit with the feeling?

PEMA: It cuts you off from your compassion and empathy for others. That gives birth to a chain reaction that causes people to self-destruct or strike out and hurt other people. It's the source of a lot of the pain and destruction that we see in the world today.

OPRAH: So what do you do to stay with it?

PEMA: I think the most straightforward way is to breathe in very deeply and connect with the feeling, and breathe it out on the exhalation. I call it compassionate abiding. It means staying with yourself when, probably for your whole lifetime, you've always run away at that point.

OPRAH: For me, that's getting a bag of chips.

PEMA: Yeah, for a lot of people, it's eating. But you could go down the list, everything from eating chips to doing some much more destructive things.

OPRAH: You wrote in *When Things Fall Apart*, "This very moment is the perfect teacher." One thing I've learned to ask, especially in difficult situations, is, "What is this here to teach me?"

PEMA: That's a very powerful way to look at it. People often use spirituality like medicine when they're in a tough situation, and they start coming up with their own ways of expressing it, as you just did. All religions point to the fact that being fully present is the only state in which you can wake up—not by somehow leaving. So you have to find your own simple, grounded language to say that to yourself, and that's a beautiful way to express it: What is this moment, this situation, or this person trying to teach me?

OPRAH: You also wrote in *When Things Fall Apart* that every day gives us an opportunity to either open up or shut down, and that the most precious opportunity presents itself when you think you can't handle whatever is happening. So if, in that moment, you can train yourself to open up instead of shutting down . . .

PEMA: That's exactly when you get a real transformation.

OPRAH: Don't you think that's hard, though? I mean, life is slamming you against a wall and you're supposed to say, "Let me open up and get slammed some more"?

PEMA: Of course it's hard. I devote my life to trying to find a way to say this so that it resonates with people. It begins with meditation—you just sit down with yourself. It's a way of being completely open to whatever is happening in your mind, and you realize your mind is wild and crazy and all over the place. The instruction is so simple: Just keep coming back to your breath. Then you say, "This is almost impossible!" It isn't, but I know how hard it is.

OPRAH: Why do Buddhists always seem so peaceful? Are you just walking around beaming love?

PEMA: I don't want to make any false statements here—

my children might read this and blow my cover! But that is my aspiration and my passion.

OPRAH: Do you ever get to have a bad day and be ticked off at people?

PEMA: Well, as much as I value my teacher, I value my family and an old friend because they don't regard me as a big deal. My son—Oprah, this was so wonderful—recently, my son very sweetly said, "Mom, tell me honestly: What does your Buddhism have to do with the fact that you get so uptight about things?" I just roared with laughter. I said, "It has nothing to do with my Buddhism at all, except that I don't flagellate myself for it." Your family and your old friends still see you as the person you always were. Without them, you could think you were pretty hot stuff.

OPRAH: What would you consider the fundamental pearl of wisdom from the teachings of the Buddha?

PEMA: Oh, my goodness! From all the fundamental pearls of wisdom . . . Can I put it in Christian terms?

OPRAH: Yes, I'll accept that.

PEMA: It would be something like "Do unto others as you would have them do unto you." Also, stay open to whatever life presents you with, because it will teach you something if you'll let it. It's about keeping an unbiased heart and mind. A lot of it is forming an unconditional friend-ship with yourself as you begin to see all the stuff you've been running away from.

OPRAH: When you asked if you could put that in Chris-tian terms, I was wondering: Can you be Christian and Buddhist at the same time?

PEMA: You can certainly be a good Christian and be completely involved in these ideas and meditation.

OPRAH: In the book *Eat Pray Love*, Elizabeth Gilbert describes how during a period of meditation, she experi-enced nirvana; she felt that she was in the palm of God's hand. Have you ever experienced anything like that?

PEMA: Yes. For me, it's lightening up about all the relative facts of life, seeing things from a much more vast and timeless perspective. That's not to say that relative things don't arise in your life, but there is a feeling of lightness about what's coming; it passes, but this timeless nowness is always here, always present, and always avail-able to everyone. According to the Buddhist belief, you can go on and on indefinitely, so you see your life as just a brief moment in time. How you relate to that moment, and how open you are, seem like the only things that matter. One of the reasons I spend a lot of time on meditation retreats is to connect with that feeling in a more ongoing way.

OPRAH: Wow. So the more you're able to be in touch with the connection to that which is higher than yourself...

PEMA: It's connecting with what is higher than the ego—that limited perspective where you become self-absorbed and it's all about "How am I looking?"

OPRAH: And "What do I have?" and "What am I doing?" and "What are other people thinking of what I'm doing? I'm separate from everybody else and I'm separate from what I think is missing, and I'm separate from God."

PEMA: That's right. It's a strong feeling of separation, even if you don't consciously recognize that. Say you're having a conversation with someone, you're interested in what they're saying, and you're right there. Then this thought crosses your mind: "Was what I just said stupid?" And you're not there anymore.

OPRAH: It takes you out of the discussion.

PEMA: And it closes you off from the amazing capacity that we have to be completely open and loving.

OPRAH: So the more you meditate...

PEMA: The more you have a lightness about what's occurring in your life. But it's not about becoming indifferent to life's experiences; it actually allows you to be much more present with whatever arises because you experience it from this timeless space. You're fully engaged, but you see it from a different perspective. One way to think of it is, at the moment of your death, how significant will winning that argument seem?

OPRAH: So when you meditate and feel the oneness and love that connect us all, it makes the other stuff in the world seem more mundane. But trying to feel that we're all connected can be hard considering how much of the conflict in our world is based on people believing that they're right and the other person or group is wrong.

PEMA: Sometimes people's spiritual ideas become fixed and they use them against those who don't share their beliefs—in effect, becoming fundamentalist. It's very dangerous—the finger of righteous indignation pointing at someone who is identified as bad or wrong. You get a lot of false security from that, and the underlying tenderheartedness that's available in all of us turns into a hard view of other people. But when you know yourself at a very deep level, you know other people. Then it's very hard to condemn them when their minds get sick or carried away by emotionality, because you've seen it in yourself.

OPRAH: It goes back to the idea of trying to manage the ego so your life isn't controlled by it. So much of the pain and suffering we all endure is because we can't keep the ego in check.

PEMA: If you're always trying to get things to work out so that it's all pleasure and no pain, then you're going to be stuck in this cycle that's doomed to failure. That belief is one of the major causes of suffering. You keep thinking, erroneously, "Well, other people have it together, and if I could just scramble enough, I could avoid all these bad feelings." But the Buddha said no, it's a myth to think that you can get all the pieces to line up so that everything goes your way. That's what I mean by being open and receptive to situations, rather than trying to control everything. The Buddha taught that we're not actually in control, which is a pretty scary idea. But when you let things be as they are, you will be a much happier, more balanced, compassionate person.

OPRAH: Which brings us back to being in the now, not resisting it or trying to change it.

PEMA: Exactly. "Being in the now" has become such a catchphrase, but it is actually very profound.

OPRAH: I loved how Eckhart Tolle redefined the present moment in his book *The Power of Now*. He said that all the stress and pain in the world is about not being in the now, because it's not allowing whatever moment you're in, even if it is a moment of despair, to be that moment; wanting it to be something else is what causes the pain and the suffering.

PEMA: That was the basic teaching of the Buddha. Not only that, but the pain that you're resisting cuts you off from understanding other people. You could say that meditation is about being receptive rather than resisting. That takes some learning, but if you're hurting enough, you'll be highly motivated to do it.

OPRAH: Ultimately, it's understanding what you conclude in *When Things Fall Apart:* that we all get so caught up in the goal, but the path itself is the goal.

PEMA: The journey is all there is, really. The future never comes, because it's always the present moment.

OPRAH: And when you know that, you get to move through the world without as much stress. What would you suggest to those of us who don't necessarily want to become Buddhists, but who do want to continue toward being as highly evolved as we can be? Meditation?

PEMA: Yes. And to notice when you're hooked, meaning something has triggered you. You're biting the hook and about to get swept away and lose being in the now.

OPRAH: What do you do when that happens?

PEMA: Notice it, pause, take three to five deep breaths. Just doing that is a shift. Then you can do something different.

OPRAH: That is beautiful, because what you said is true—the moment you realize whatever it is that triggers you or hooks you, in taking those deep breaths, you change your vibrational frequency and allow for the possibility of something better to happen.

PEMA: Yes. When you're triggered and you take those conscious breaths, you begin to understand that if you keep talking to yourself, you're fueling the triggered feeling. That feeling comes with an undertow; you're going to get swept away again and end up with the same result.

OPRAH: But if you pause and breathe, you open the door to bring something new in.

PEMA: Yes. And you open yourself up to infinite possibilities.

The End of the Despair

Will Boast

Seven years ago, I was stranded—grief-stricken, a year out of grad school, living alone in a rented house in Virginia. My dad had passed away, and I'd sold our family home in Wisconsin. The last anchor to my past was gone; the future spread before me like an ocean, blank and formless. I made lists of places I might go, wrote out pros and cons. But there seemed no point in going anywhere at all.

I filled my time with books. One night I sat down to finish Graham Greene's *The End of the Affair*, the story of a love triangle: Henry, a London civil servant, is married to Sarah, who takes as her lover Bendrix, a young writer. The novel, set in the darkest days of World War II, is also a story of faith. When Bendrix's flat is hit by a bomb, Sarah asks God to let him live. Moments later, Bendrix emerges from the debris; in the end, it's Sarah who dies. Henry and Bendrix, former rivals, are united by loss. Henry invites Bendrix to move in with him, and the bereaved men make a home together. Upon finishing Greene's book, I was unaccountably comforted. That night I slept better than I had in weeks.

The next morning, I was awakened by a call from a childhood friend. He'd just broken up with his girlfriend of six years. He wanted me to come to Madison and move in with him, help him make rent. Maybe he needed me to see him through the breakup. I knew I needed him to help me come back to life.

He flew down to Virginia so we could take shifts driving the moving van to Wisconsin. I packed my things, still slightly bewildered at how it had all come to pass.

On the morning we pulled out of town, I was driving through my residential neighborhood when I saw a figure emerge from the mist: a massive black-and-white creature on four hooves. It was a Holstein cow, the very emblem of America's Dairyland. It passed within feet of us, then disappeared into a backyard. There were no farms for miles.

"I'll never lose my faith in coincidence," Bendrix says in Greene's novel.

There are rare moments when life, often so arbitrary, sends you a note of encouragement. *You can put your faith in friends*, it said that day. *You can find your way*.

I like to think we followed that cow all the way back home.

The Hardest Question

Chris Adrian

As a divinity student, I spend my time in a state of near-perpetual confusion. I have not read a tenth of what my classmates have. Immanuel Kant and Friedrich Schleiermacher were the friends of their youth the way the Bionic Woman and Marie Osmond were the friends of mine. And my theological vocabulary, compared with that of my peers, is so impoverished as to make me practically a divine mute.

During my second semester, I took a course on literature and theology, and at one of the first few sessions I woke from a daydream to discover that my classmates were eagerly discussing the *Odyssey*. I panicked, figuring that even though for once I had done the reading, I had done the wrong reading. But when I fiddled in my notebook to check the syllabus, the *Odyssey* was nowhere to be found. I poked my neighbor at the seminar table, gently, in the ribs. "We were supposed to read the *Odyssey*?"

"Huh?" she said. "What are you talking about?" When I'm not in class, I work as a pediatrician, and I noticed pretty early that though divinity school, like pediatrics, is full of largehearted, patient people, during intense intellectual discussions my fellow students can get a little testy.

"Why are we talking about the *Odyssey*?"

"Not the *Odyssey*," she said. "The Odyssey. Leibniz. Bayle. Polkinghorne. Those guys."

"Oh," I said, but she could tell I was still confused, so she wrote the word on my notebook, which was blank except for a half-finished doodle of a pony.

Theodicy.

"Oh," I said, as if I recognized the word. The class discussion moved on without my ever deciphering what exactly they were talking about—everyone lamenting the problem of theodicy without ever saying what it was—so I walked to the library after class to consult the dictionary and discovered that, like anyone who has ever felt afflicted by existence, I was already familiar with the concept, if not the word. It means an attempt to reconcile a God who is thoroughly and supremely good with the undeniable fact of evil in the world. It was as strange and embarrassing as the episode in class had been, to stand there and learn a word I suddenly felt I should have known all my life.

You don't have to have your cookies stolen in kindergarten too many times before you start to perceive that all is not right with the world. My cookies were stolen so often that I learned to offer them before they were demanded; my tormentor was a girl whose name I have long forgotten but whose face, round and sweet and utterly at odds with her dreadful disposition, has remained with me forever. I was raised Catholic but was at that age more a dreamy little pagan, and it was indicative of my particular brand of religiosity that I prayed to Big Bird and not to Jesus to deliver me from my freckled oppressor. When nothing changed, I continued to believe in Big Bird, but I gave up on the notion that he cared very specifically about what happened to me.

As I became an older child and then a teenager, and dogs died and family members died and did not return to life no matter how hard I prayed, I reconciled miserable reality with faith in an all-powerful and entirely benevolent God by telling myself that it wasn't that God didn't care to intervene or didn't have the power to—my grief was just too particular to attract his attention. And as I grew still older and began to notice that we are accompanied throughout history by all sorts of unspeakable suffering, I amended this view, too, telling myself that the sum of these miserable parts must add up to something I could never apprehend while alive, and that although the fact of evil in the world might speak against God's scrutability, it said nothing about his existence or beneficence. But the older I became, and the more unhappy a place the world revealed itself to be, the more difficult it became to accept the idea of a personally invested, personally loving God.

Most days it's not the most pressing question in the world—how God can be good and allow terrible things to occur. It's when something really bad happens to you, or collective cataclysm descends, or some really wretched piece of news falls out of the television or slithers from the papers, that this question that has vexed generations becomes all of a sudden quite present and personal. I would venture to guess that there are certain obsessive sorts of personalities who dwell on it even on sunny days and during Disney ice shows (maybe even especially during Disney ice shows), but for people with certain jobs—theologian, divinity student, detective, physician—it becomes a professional hazard. By the time I got to residency, I understood that I needed to come up with an answer to the question people kept asking when I told them I wanted to be a pediatric oncologist: "How can you stand to work in a field where you see such terrible things?"

I did see terrible things, but in fact it was those terrible things that seemed to enable me to get up and go back to work every day. If the parents and children who were actually suffering with the illnesses could be as gracious as I discovered them to be, the very least I could do was get myself back to the hospital to be with them as they labored through the process of getting well or dying. Sometimes it seemed that the failure of drugs or technology reduced the practice of medicine to a ministry of accompaniment. I say reduced, but you could argue that it's an elevation of our practice as physicians. I came to divinity school largely because I thought the experience and education would make me better able to accompany patients into their adversity, and I think I'm in the right place for that. But it turns out that I have already learned things as a doctor that make me if not a smarter divinity student, at least a less agitated one.

Every parent and child I meet who overcomes or succumbs to illness is challenged to reconcile their fate with their faith in the goodness of the world. They never reason or parse like theologians, and by no means do they all express a faith in any kind of God, but they all find strength and will to wake up every day to a job tremendously more difficult than mine. A child complains one morning at the breakfast table of numbness in one arm and then collapses from a catastrophic cerebral bleed (or pulls a steaming rice cooker down upon her head, or rides a scooter headfirst into a speeding taxi), and a parent's world suddenly collapses. It's a privilege and a burden to be witness to other people's tragedies, to watch them proceed from stunned disbelief to miserable acknowledgment to stoic acceptance and then beyond to the place I can't quite enter myself, a place in which they are both fully aware of how completely horrible life can be and yet still fully in love with it, possessed of a particular buoyancy of spirit that is somehow heavier than it is light.

I can't say if I believe in the God who knows us and cares for us down to the last hair on our head, and so I don't feel obligated to reconcile such a being with the ugly facts of the chromosomal syndrome trisomy 13, or teenage myelogenous leukemia, but I am pretty sure one need look no further than people's responses to adversity to find evidence that there is something in the world that resists tragedy and seeks to overturn the evils of seeming fate.

The last and least of my professions, after physician and student, is fiction writer, and I'd like to think that the little tragedy-resisting organ in me is the one that generates stories. They are ghastly, depressing stories for the most part, about ghosts, and zombies, and unhappy angels managing apocalypses, and people attempting to bring the dead back to life, but they are a great comfort to me. I write fiction mostly to try to make sense of my own petty and profound misery, and I fail every time, but every time I come away with a peculiar sort of contentment, as if it were just the trying that mattered. And maybe that's the best answer to the patently ridiculous problem of trying to reconcile all the very visible evil and suffering in the world with the existence of a God who is not actually out to get us: We suffer and we don't give up.

Everything Is Illuminated

Naomi Barr

My mother never wanted anyone to have to take care of her. "Just send me out on an ice floe," she'd say. In the five years she had non-Hodgkin's lymphoma, she went to chemo, shopped for wigs, managed her insurance bills, and still made herb-stuffed chicken nearly every week for her and my dad. Then, abruptly, her oncologist said there was nothing more they could do. Two, maybe three months, he said.

Within a week, she no longer had the energy to shop or cook. She would sit in a chair, holding her head, staring and thinking.

It was a Sunday when she collapsed while walking upstairs. Hospice set up a bed in the den, where a wall of windows looked onto the snow-covered yard. On Tuesday, an aide taught me how to roll her from one side to the other to change the sheets. On Wednesday, a nurse showed me how to place a syringe between her cheek and molars so the bitter-tasting morphine could drip down her throat.

I'd shared nearly everything with my mom—probably too much. She could turn the knife, but she was usually right, and she loved me no matter what. She was the person I called when I broke up with a boyfriend ("He was wet behind the ears," she said) and when my first article got published ("Mazel tov! Now keep writing"). Sometimes I called simply to hear her voice.

And now I couldn't make her better the way she'd made me better. I read her Shakespeare and Robert Burns, but she struggled to stay awake. I made ice pops out of grape juice, crushed them, and spoon-fed her the pieces, but by Friday she could no longer swallow. No matter what I did, my mother was going to die.

When I was little, after my mom had tucked me in, I'd close my eyes, hold my breath, and try to imagine death. The thought scared me so badly, I'd scream, "I don't want to die!" and run to her.

As I watched her sleep, I wondered whether I could bear being in the room when it happened.

One week after her initial collapse, she slipped into unconsciousness. My sisters and I stayed up through the night, watching for the signs that the end was near: Her breathing became shallow. Her skin was cold. Her extremities had gone purple. The room was silent, save the hum of the oxygen machine; early morning light filled the space. My mother was still. There was no more attempting to move her, no more coming and going. Nothing needed to be done.

"We should say the Sh'ma for her," my oldest sister said. The Sh'ma is a Hebrew prayer that is supposed to be the last thing a Jew utters before dying. Because my mom could no longer speak, we spoke it for her.

Then my sister whispered, "You're also supposed to open a window to allow the spirit to leave." My mom didn't believe in an afterlife, but we cracked open a window just in case, then repeated the Sh'ma on the off chance she'd heard us talking.

I held her hand. Her breathing became slower, like a mechanical toy whose mechanism has begun to wind down. I watched as delicate breaths caught in her mouth—

an inhale, a pause, an exhale, an inhale, a longer pause, an exhale. Then nothing. I stared for several seconds before I understood that I'd just witnessed my mother's last moment on earth.

I had imagined she would say a final word. But her passing was no less profound for its silence. As I watched the woman who gave birth to me die, the unknown became known. I had the answer I'd wanted since I was a little girl: *Death is a part of life.*

I thought the mother I'd relied upon had left us earlier that week. I thought she'd offered all the wisdom, all the comfort, she could. But I was wrong. Even with her last breath, she still had more to give.

Strength from Within

Hold up your head! . . . You were made for victory.

—ANNE GILCHRIST

With Love

Brenda Shaughnessy

Before the birth of my son six years ago, I would have defined strength as a gruff grinning and bearing, the opposite of uncertainty. When he was born with severe brain damage and later diagnosed with cerebral palsy, I felt anything but strong. I was devastated. But I promised myself that I would find a way to handle whatever happened. My baby boy deserved and needed nothing less.

I came to see that what constitutes strength is not just muscle or will. It can also include the most desperate vulnerability, the saddest heartache, the lightest, sweetest laughter. Being strong for my son meant learning to love not just him but his endless crying, too. It meant letting my lovely flesh-and-blood child take the place of my abstract fears. It meant accepting those fears as the flip side of my love, my weakness as part of my resolve.

He couldn't latch on or breast-feed; he wasn't holding up his head; he wailed mightily and furiously for no reason we knew. He did not smile or laugh. He might never see, walk, or talk. Yet he was also this marvelous red-haired, chubby-cheeked, green-blue-gold-eyed baby who could, I absolutely knew, feel my love and return it. My child was both the light of my life and the nexus of my deepest worry, and I had to be strong enough to accept this paradox.

One day, at long last, I saw him smile back, recognizing me and feeling—I swear he sighed with pleasure—safe and happy in my arms. I knew for certain that he was aware of how loved and adored and wanted he was, and that steeled me for the years of caretaking to follow. Through surgeries, therapies, and medications, no one has smiled like this boy. I try to remember how brave he is, because this bright-eyed, vibrant child is a source, not just a recipient, of love.

People are always complimenting parents of children with special needs—for being *so amazingly strong*. But it doesn't take strength to love your child. Love gives you resilience. When I tend to my disabled child's medical needs, I'm simply being a mom, caring for my son. Strength means honoring your entire range of emotion, even your despair and heartbreak. *Especially* your despair and heartbreak. It means acknowledging each of those feelings, your questions and ideas and faith and terror, and meeting what comes with the full force of your heart.

Off the Beating Path

Martha Beck

"What is happening to my life?" said Dorothy, exhaustedly sipping a triple espresso across the table from me. "Did I do something to deserve this?"

By "this," Dorothy meant a series of crises that had recently hit her like a gang of meth-crazed prizefighters. Her husband had filed for divorce—a week after she lost her job, the same day she was diagnosed with diabetes. Then her best friend moved away. Now Dorothy was caring for both her aging parents while paying a divorce lawyer way more than she (or her retirement account) could afford. "I'm not sure I can go on," she told me. "Why is all this happening at once?"

"Well," I said, "according to probability theory, random events can run in streaks. It's like patterned disorder, and in nature it creates beautiful things."

Dorothy looked as though I'd poured mouse droppings into her coffee. "That's your explanation? My screwed-up life is just beautifully random?"

"It's the most rational explanation," I said. "It's not my explanation."

"What is?"

I shrugged. "I think you've hit a rumble strip."

Then I laid out for Dorothy what I'll now lay out for you, just in case your own current luck makes Job look like a lottery winner. I don't know why catastrophes sometimes come in clusters. But experience and observation have convinced me that these patches of awfulness may be purposeful and, in the end, benevolent. If you've had a run of horrible luck, you can tell yourself you're being tortured or punished. Or you can decide you're being steered.

Imagine that your true self is your essential consciousness, the part of you that still feels what it was like to be you ten years ago, even though most of the atoms in your physical body have been replaced since then. Suppose you set out to experience the adventure of human life by inhabiting your body. And that this essential you sees your life as an epic road trip. Destination: inner wisdom, love, and joy.

Now let's suppose you forgot this destiny at birth. In its place you created a mental map of the life route you preferred—passing through good health, perfect romance, and professional success on the way to a cheery, painless death (say, being struck by a meteorite while bicycling at the age of 110).

Unfortunately, your essential self very probably has in mind a stranger and more exciting road, featuring spooky tunnels, scary precipices, and sharp curves. Which means your destiny isn't at all what you think you want. Which means that as you drive along the road of life, there will be times when your essential self plans to turn even though you most certainly do not.

Maybe you planned to become a dentist and marry your high school boyfriend, only to realize that (1) you hate staring into other people's mouths, and (2) you actually prefer women. So you quit dental school, break up with Mr. Wrong, and find work and love that suit your innate preferences.

Or not. This is a best-case scenario, and such scenarios virtually never happen.

What virtually always happens is that when destiny swerves, we proceed straight ahead. We step on the gas, ignoring the fact that we feel trapped in the dead relationship, stifled by the secure job. We go blind to the landscape and the road signs, steering by our assumptions about what life should be, as unaware of those assumptions as a sleeping driver is of her unconsciousness.

I call them rumble strips.

I hit my first one while driving hell-for-leather toward my third Harvard degree. In six memorable months, I was almost killed in a car accident, in a high-rise fire, and by a violent autoimmune reaction to an accidental pregnancy. I had incessant nausea. And fibromyalgia. And lice. By the time the baby was diagnosed with Down syndrome, I was pretty much done for.

It took all that to shatter my core assumption: that achievement and intellect gave my life its value. Only after my world seemed to completely fall apart did I learn the lesson my true self needed me to learn: that no brass ring is worth a damn compared with the one thing that makes life worth living—love. Duh. You'd think I'd have figured that out earlier. There were signs absolutely everywhere. But until my first rumble strip shook me awake, I never even noticed them.

I've had other streaks of awful "luck" since, but none has ever caused as much suffering. That's because I've developed a rumble-strip coping strategy. If your own luck seems weirdly cursed, try this:

STEP 1: Hit the brakes.

When Dorothy told me over coffee that she wasn't sure she could go on, I secretly rejoiced—not because I wanted her to suffer, but because I didn't.

"Yup," I said, trying not to sound smug. "The rumble strip is telling you to stop."

"Stop what?"

"Everything," I told her. "Except what's necessary to survive. Eat. Sleep. Go to the bathroom. Make sure your children, pets, and sick parents eat, sleep, and go to the bathroom. If that's beyond you, ask for help. Not forever. Just for now."

This time Dorothy looked as though I'd asked her to stab a baby panda, but she was too exhausted to argue. That was a good thing. When you feel so beaten down that you can't sustain normal activities, it's time to stop trying. Surrender, Dorothy.

STEP 2: Put your mind in reverse.

From a place of minimal functioning, you can back off the rumble strip—by reversing the assumptions that steered you onto it in the first place. These key assumptions are clearly marked with intense negative emotions: fear, anger, sadness. Such feelings are big red WRONG WAY signs. Back away from them.

To help Dorothy do this, I asked her which, of all her tribulations, was causing her the most pain. Topping her very long list was the thought "My marriage has failed." So that's where we began shifting Dorothy's mind into reverse.

"Give me three reasons your marriage actually didn't fail," I said.

"But it did!" Dorothy muffled a sob.

"Well, was any part of it good?"

"Yes. Of course."

"Did you learn from it?"

"I learned so much," said Dorothy.

"And is every learning experience that comes to an end a failure?" I asked. "Like school, or childhood, or life?"

"Well, no."

Dorothy paused, thinking. Then her shoulders relaxed just a little. Ta-da! She'd begun reversing a painful assumption.

To be clear, I wasn't trying to minimize Dorothy's pain or plaster a creepy happy face over her legitimate sorrow. I only wanted her to alter her beliefs enough to catch a glimpse of a different road, where a marriage could succeed as a soul adventure even if it didn't last forever.

Try throwing your mind into reverse right now. Think of the worst, most hurtful thing that's happening in your life. Now think of a way this horrible thing might be good. The more rigidly you hold on to your assumptions, the harder this process will be. But with practice you'll improve—and trust me, it's so worth the effort. When life gets rumbly, being able to reverse an assumption turns out to be the handiest skill imaginable.

STEP 3: Find and follow smooth terrain.

Because rumble strips are one of the few experiences that will make sensible people hire a life coach, I've been privy to hundreds of them. And I've noticed a very consistent pattern: At the point when someone sees through a false assumption, the road of life suddenly turns smooth.

Instead of crazy bad luck, bits of strangely good luck start showing up. They're small at first, inconspicuous. Never mind—slather them with attention. Your attention is what steers your life, and it's much more pleasant to steer by focusing on the good stuff.

In Dorothy's case, the moment she reversed her assumption that divorce always means failure, the waitress brought her a cupcake, said, "On the house," and walked away. Later that afternoon, Dorothy found an abandoned *New York Times* unfolded to an article titled "The Good Divorce," which helped and encouraged her. Then she ran into a former boyfriend she hadn't seen in years. During their brief interaction, he told her how much he still respected her and how valuable their "failed" relationship still was to him.

Little miracles like this will begin happening to you whenever you turn toward your right life, even if you're in the middle of a rumble strip. If you stop everything you think you should be doing, surrender to what's actually happening, reverse your assumptions, and steer toward the glimmers of light that appear as your old beliefs shatter, the small miracles will turn into big ones. Eventually, your good luck will seem as incredible and mysterious as your bad. Once more you'll be asking, "Did I do something to deserve this?" Only this time, the question will arise from a sense of overwhelming gratitude, not overwhelming pain.

By the way, the answer to that question is yes. You did do something to deserve this. You had the courage to keep traveling the precarious road of life. You deserve to be guided. And rewarded. And, when all else fails, rumbled.

Join the Party

Zoe Donaldson

Six years ago, on a blustery Maine night, in my college's dingy theater—which was sardine packed with peers, professors, a handful of confused locals, and Sigourney Weaver—I performed an experimental art piece in my underwear. I've also belted (okay, yodeled) Alanis Morissette numbers in karaoke bars from Spain to Colorado, given impromptu toasts at countless parties ("Even when I played a prostitute, Grandma always supported my acting...."), and been first on the dance floor for as long as I can recall. (Last summer I was also first to split my pants on said dance floor.) I'm not immune to fear, but for me the rewards of being bold have always surpassed the risks.

Through all the speeches, splits, and soaring renditions

of "Son of a Preacher Man," I've never had any trouble exposing my good, my bad, and my seriously ugly, because each of these feats brought me closer to someone, or even a lot of someones. What makes these memories so special, so vibrant, are the good folks I shared them with—the laughs I had with friends, the hands that lifted me (and helped me find a new pair of pants). Opening yourself up can inspire others to do the same. I'm the first to dip it low—but it's never long before others eagerly follow suit.

You may never get to publicly disrobe for Sigourney Weaver, but that's not exactly the point. Yes, my comfort zone happens to be as big as Texas, but I imagine there are circumstances when you feel safe enough to reveal your inner entertainer—and trust me, she's in there. Let me gently nudge you toward the microphone by reminding you that with every act of bravery comes the chance to experience something spectacular: joy, hilarity, kindness, love, connection. It's not a foolproof equation; there's no guarantee. All I really have is a hypothesis based on anecdotal evidence. But I bet you'll have a lot of fun testing it out.

After He Left

Suzanne Finnamore

One day your husband says he isn't happy. If you are like most women, if you are like me, you roll up your sleeves and say, "I can fix this." You try to make him happy. You let him go out with his friends more often, you give him an icy martini at the end of his day, you rub his shoulders, you do not confront him on any issues—say, your own unhappiness. You do a Perfect Wife impersonation and, piece by piece, you give away what you were.

It doesn't work.

Then one day he says he may want to consider a separation. You know then that he is overworked and is certainly overreacting to something you have said or done. You cry; you say, "What about the baby?" He backs down, but the words are out there. You can't see them, but like carbon monoxide, they have quietly entered your home and are doing their sad work.

Eventually, the topic of divorce is broached. Then, of course, you beg for a separation. But it's too late. Now he wants a divorce; now he has a lawyer—something no one wants her husband to have. Having a lawyer means he probably has been thinking about this for a very, very long time. Whereas you've only just started thinking about it, only just grasped the reality as you watch him pack his suitcases and leave.

He says, "You should receive the papers in a few days." The door shuts quietly behind him.

You would think this would make it real. But for me, it didn't.

The doorbell seems to ring and ring and ring. I open the door to find a small brown-haired woman.

"Are you Suzanne Finnamore?"

"Yes, I am," I say. At least I think I am. I seem to have momentarily left my body.

She hands me a thick white legal-size envelope with my

name handwritten on it. I know inside this envelope there is not a coupon for a free salad with a large pizza or an invitation to a fund-raiser for Guatemala. For once, I would do anything if she were from the Sierra Club. I would kill for a Jehovah's Witness. The roses in the front yard have misunderstood and have chosen this very day to begin to bloom: a pinkness in the periphery of my vision.

"Can I sign this and just give it back to you now?" I ask.

"No," she says. "You have to read it before you sign."

I rarely read anything before I sign it. This is, of course, one of my problems. The most recent of which is divorce.

I cry for days on end. I cry until my eyes look like a prizefighter's—one who has lost badly. I talk to my best friend and my mother several times a day. "How am I going to get through this?" I ask. "You will," they say. "You're strong."

"I'm not," I say. "You don't know."

I go into my son's room, and while I am changing his diaper, I wipe tears away, a fake smile on my face. "Mommy has a cold," I say. "Cold!" he says, laughing. I thank God that he is so young, and then I cry because he is so young. I cry when he looks around the room and says, "Da Da?"

"I want to die," I say to my mother.

"Believe me, you won't," she assures me while sipping a Diet Coke on my couch. "You are going to go on and be happy."

"How do you know?" I ask.

"I did," she says simply. And, of course, she did. My father left home when I was seven; my mother remarried and has been with the same man for thirty years.

"You got the last good one," I say.

"That's your grief talking," she says.

My grief over this divorce is not just talking, it is screaming in my ear twenty-four hours a day.

I sleep with him again. I say to him, "Didn't you think this was going to happen?"

"No," he says with a puzzled look on his face, as if he had just found a whole walnut inside a box of Cracker Jack.

"Well, I did," I say.

He rubbed my back, is how it started. What was he doing in my bedroom at seven A.M.? Well, yes, I did call him at six A.M. You see, I'd had chills and a fever the night before, and I called him to come right away and take care of the baby. Unfortunately, the fever and chills disappeared when he arrived in a flannel shirt. Flannel shirts should be outlawed for ex-husbands. Flannel shirts are to women what crotchless panties are to men.

I report this to my best friend, Mae. I feel bad, as though I were two years sober and had chugged a pint of Jack Daniel's. I tell her, "But I just wanted to have sex."

"Oh, I know," she says. "I know, girl."

"The weird thing is," I say, "we're still married."

"I can't even imagine," she says. "Is he taking advantage of you?" Actually she says, "He's taking advantage of you."

"I know," I say. "I'm going to stop." And I do.

There is no one in the house I have to try to make happy. There are no more arguments or nights when I turn away from him in quiet despair as he snores, loneliness folding me in its chill arms. There is no more doubt creeping up my spine and squeezing my heart; crippling my brain, which has been sending me messages like *Get out. Stop.*

I am no longer running to the door in crisp cotton clothes to see his fake smile when he arrives home with the grimace of a man who is about to pull the rip cord on his parachute. I would have to try to please, try to please, try to please. Would you like pork chops for dinner? How about steak? Is the rice all right? As though the right food would make him suddenly smite his forehead and say, "Damn, you're great! I'd marry you all over again tomorrow."

I have hung up my have-a-nice-day mask. He is never going to have a nice day while he is with me. I am not a conduit to his nice day. But I have gotten so good at it, the pleasing disease, that it seems a shame to stop now. Actually, I don't have to. I can please myself. I put away the tight lingerie, the bright patter, the mascara.

My face looks plain but clean. In the mirror, it looks like me again. The fear has left my eyes.

I am reclaiming my home. Everything stays a lot neater. The toilet seat is perpetually down. I have the remote control to the television: No one can take that away. Also, I can let myself go. No, I cannot hang from chandeliers, intoxicated with my own hilarity, but at dusk when the baby is asleep I can turn off the television and listen to the birds.

I think about the good times, what I think of as my real

marriage, not this recent hell. I must say, the benefits of divorce do not begin to rival the benefits of my real marriage yet, but it is early. I try to withhold judgment. But divorce, I have to admit, is way out in front of the way the past six months have been. Okay, I admit it: the past year.

I cry quite a bit still. This, of course, is not a benefit. But it is the only way I know to feel better. Rain on the prairie.

Now so many events and moments that had seemed insignificant add up. I remember how for Valentine's Day he gave me flowers but no card. I remember how when we ate in restaurants, he looked off into the middle distance while my hand was creeping across the table to hold his. He would always let go first.

As in all times of crisis, I read poetry. Theodore Roethke: "In a dark time, the eye begins to see."

And this is true: I do see more. I see that I had not been happy either. I remember thinking one desolate Sunday night, Is this how I am going to spend the rest of my life? Married to someone who is perpetually distracted and somewhat wistful, as though a marvelous party is going on in the next room, which but for me he could be attending?

I read love poetry, and that makes me very quiet. I decide not to read love poetry for a while.

Since all of this began, I have lost twenty-six pounds. I can wear my size 9/10 black bikini again. It is a benefit. I chalk it up. When people see me, they say, "You look great."

I say, "My husband left me."

They say, "Oh, no."

"Oh, yes," I say. I have to admit, that's kind of fun. Being able to surprise people.

I do not eat very often. When I do eat, it is things with extra fat and sugar. I have two Chips Ahoy! cookies at the end of each day: my reward for not hanging myself with a bra in our two-car garage, which now has only one car. (Another benefit: I can park sloppily.)

I am saving scads of money at the supermarket. I no longer buy meat, no thick rib-eye steaks or turkey-basil sausages. My refrigerator is crammed with old condiments, meat and condiments being the mainstays of most men. But I have no man now. I am like a movie: *No Man of Her Own*. I feel demoted and also something else that I cannot quite admit to myself: liberated.

I get the idea to have my engagement ring sized to a pinkie ring. I return to the man who originally sold it to us. I remove my sunglasses and look him straight in the eye. "Can you size this to my pinkie finger," I say. It is not a question.

He says, "Are you sure you don't want a pendant?"

This is not his first divorce.

"I don't wear pendants," I say.

"You look great," he says.

"Thank you," I say. I know it is true. I keep my head high as I leave the store. Then I enter the street and begin to sob.

On the way home, I pass a church where a bride and groom are just emerging. They seem like children wandering into the woods. I hope this feeling will pass. I would like to believe in marriage again, someday. Today, I realize, is not the day.

For a while, I take small pleasure in the fact that a famous actor is divorcing his famous actress wife. If he can divorce this famous actress, who is stunning and sexy and smart besides, then maybe this whole thing is all right.

Then two nights later, as I am watching TV, I learn that the famous actor has withdrawn his petition for divorce.

"Damn," I say. I am in front of the television eating Kentucky Fried Chicken. I have not bathed in two days. Still, I had identified with the famous actress. But that is all over now. I feel stunned at this news.

Then I do something I haven't done in months. I have a good laugh.

You Look Fine

Celia Barbour

I knew how I was supposed to look, and that I didn't measure up. My sources were, on the one hand, *Charlie's Angels* and, on the other, the hallway mirror, which testified to the inadequacy of my thirteen-year-old body.

"I'm so fat and ugly no one's ever going to like me," I moaned to my mother.

She was not alarmed. She said, almost scoldingly, "You look fine. You are *not* fat. Sit up straight and finish your breakfast."

Clearly, she was blind. I embarked on a jogging regimen, awakening in the darkness to put on my Adidas, slipping out of the house. When I returned, my father barely looked up from his oatmeal. "If you want exercise, there's plenty of lawn to be mowed," he said.

My parents' obtuseness antagonized me. Instead of helping me overcome my freakishness, they pretended not to see it. To them, exercise was frivolous; dieting was frivolous. The whole pursuit of beauty—makeup, blow-dryers, my beloved *Mademoiselle* magazine that explained step by step how to create a smoldering eye—was a huge, scandalous waste of energy. I longed with the deep hunger of the malnourished to experience prettiness in all its artificially enhanced forms. But I couldn't even walk through the kitchen with blush on my cheeks without drawing their quiet censure.

In those days, my father was a professor at a liberal arts college. His colleagues had shaggy hair and dressed in smocks made by Guatemalan peasants, or dandruff epaulets on their thrift store suits. The only people who dolled up their faces and feathered their hair were the townies, and they were not worth emulating. The prevailing attitude on campus was clear: You worried about your appearance only if you had nothing better to contribute to the world. If you were talented, brilliant, funny, or wise, you were free to ignore superficial things, like beauty.

Eventually I emerged into a kind of quiet prettiness. It suited me fine. I was never drop-dead stunning, but I went out with the boys I had crushes on. It was a happy way to spend my late teens and twenties.

Now I am forty-four and once again do not love the mirror. In it I see a body stretched and battered by the birth of three children, a face turning wrinkled and gray. And I think, Yuck. But I also think, Well, okay, I'm forty-four. Prettiness was mine when it should have been mine. Now I have other things to attend to.

Sometimes I still wish I were a little more skilled with the eyeliner, but I don't despair. I've realized that my parents' seeming cluelessness was actually great wisdom; they valued my accomplishments more than my looks. And this freed me up to discover a really important secret: The things that make me feel like a superhero—making love, swimming across a lake, staying up all night to write, giving birth to a baby—make me look like tangled, puffy hell. But the mirror can't take away what I know in my heart to be true: At times like these, I'm drop-dead gorgeous.

Your Inner Crone

Elizabeth Gilbert

Many years ago, when I was going through a dark season of depression and self-loathing, I taped a sweet photograph of myself at the tender age of two on my bathroom mirror. Looking at that photo every day reminded me that I once was this blameless little person, deserving of all tenderness—and that part of me would always be this blameless little person deserving of all tenderness. Meditating upon a smaller and more innocent version of my face helped me learn to be more compassionate to myself. I was finally able to recognize that any harm I inflicted on me, I was also inflicting on her. And that little kid clearly didn't deserve to be harmed.

Reconnecting with one's inner child is a terrific therapeutic practice, whether you have old wounds to heal or simply want to avoid opening up new ones.

These days, however, I find I'm not so interested in my inner child. Instead, I have become absolutely fixated upon channeling my "inner crone"—the badass old lady who already dwells somewhere deep within me and whom I hope to fully become someday.

I recently tucked away the photo of my adorable two-year-old self and replaced it with a photo of my favorite and most inspiring true-life crone—an elderly but sturdy Ukrainian babushka named Hanna Zavorotnya, who has a face like boiled pierogi and lives in Chernobyl. Yes, that Chernobyl.

Thirty years ago, when the nearby nuclear reactor blew up, Hanna's town became unlivable, even deadly. (And so it will remain for centuries.) The entire population was evacuated and sent to soul-crushing government housing in other cities. But as time passed, a small handful of tough peasants defiantly sneaked back to their contaminated ancestral homeland, where they have been thriving now for years. Most are in their seventies and eighties. Most—like Hanna, my human spirit animal—are women.

You know why Hanna wants to live in Chernobyl?

Because she likes it there. It's home. Is it safe? Of course not. It's some of the most dangerous land on earth. But to a lady like Hanna, who has already been through so many trials (famine, World War II, an atomic meltdown, aging itself), what does "safe" even mean anymore? So Hanna drinks the contaminated water, plants vegetable gardens in the poisoned soil, makes her own moonshine, laughs about life, and then goes outside to butcher another radioactive pig to make radioactive sausage. She is joined by her friends, who live and laugh and butcher their own irradiated pigs.

And get this: These fearless babushkas of Chernobyl are outliving their compatriots who stayed behind in the "safe" and "nontoxic" cities. Why are these tough old crones thriving? Because they are happy. And why are they happy?

Because they do exactly what they want.

I'd really like to do that.

Some might consider the word *crone* derogatory. I don't. The crone is an ancient and formidable character in myth and folklore. She's the bearer of great wisdom. Even when blind, she manages to possess supernatural vision. She is often a guardian of the underworld because she has no fear of death—which means, of course, she has no fear of anything.

We live in a society that fetishizes youth. In fact, we live in a culture where staying young is considered a real accomplishment. But I'm losing interest (if I ever had any at all) in being forever twenty-one.

Of course I still have an inner child. I always will. But these days, when my inner child starts feeling insecure or terrified of the world, I just ask myself, WWMICD? What would my inner crone do?

Then that beautiful old being rises up, fixes me with her fearless, cloudy gaze, and says the same powerful word every time: "Live."

Contributors

Chris Adrian, a pediatric oncologist, is the author of several works of fiction, including the novels *The Children's Hospital* and *The Great Night*.

Julia Alvarez has published many works of fiction, nonfiction, and poetry, including the novels *How the García Girls Lost Their Accents* and *In the Time of Butterflies*. She was the recipient of a 2013 National Medal of Arts.

Katie Arnold-Ratliff, *O, The Oprah Magazine*'s articles editor, is the author of the novel *Bright Before Us*.

Alex Banner is the owner of Wishbone Woodworking and Banner Furniture in Brooklyn, New York.

Celia Barbour, a writer, editor, and cook, lives with her family in a small town on the Hudson River. Her food writing has twice been nominated for a James Beard Award.

Naomi Barr is *O, The Oprah Magazine*'s chief of research.

Martha Beck is a life coach who has been a columnist at *O, The Oprah Magazine* since 2001. Her books include *Leaving the Saints, Finding Your Own North Star, The Joy Diet, Steering by Starlight, Finding Your Way in a Wild New World*, and, most recently, the novel *Diana, Herself.*

Aimee Bender is the author of five books, most recently *The Particular Sadness of Lemon Cake* and *The Color Master.*

Maeve Binchy (1940–2012) was the author of numerous novels, including *Circle of Friends* and *Tara Road.*

Will Boast has published two books, including the memoir *Epilogue*, a *New York Times* best seller. He is also the author of a forthcoming novel, *Daphne*.

Pema Chödrön, a Tibetan Buddhist nun, is the director of Gampo Abbey in Cape Breton, Nova Scotia, and the author of several books, including *When Things Fall Apart*.

Kelly Corrigan has written three memoirs: *The Middle Place*, *Lift*, and *Glitter and Glue*. She lives in the San Francisco Bay Area.

Edwidge Danticat, the recipient of a MacArthur Fellowship and the Langston Hughes Medal, is the author of numerous books, including *Claire of the Sea Light; Breath, Eyes, Memory;* and *The Dew Breaker*.

Kristy Davis is a writer in Brooklyn, New York.

Zoe Donaldson is *O, The Oprah Magazine*'s associate editor.

Nora Ephron (1941–2012) was a novelist, essayist, and Academy Award–nominated screenwriter whose films included *When Harry Met Sally* and *Sleepless in Seattle*.

Suzanne Finnamore has written two novels, as well as *Split: A Memoir of Divorce*. She lives with her husband and three children in North Carolina.

Ian Frazier writes nonfiction, essays, and humor. He has published a dozen books and has twice won the Thurber Prize for American Humor. He lives in Montclair, New Jersey.

Lise Funderburg is a writer and editor based in Philadelphia, Pennsylvania.

Mary Gaitskill has published six works of fiction, most recently the novel *The Mare*.

Elizabeth Gilbert is the author, most recently, of *Big Magic: Creative Living Beyond Fear*, as well as six other books, including the memoir *Eat Pray Love*, which sold more than a million copies.

Alexandra Harney, an economist and Reuters' special correspondent for China, is the author of *The China Price: The True Cost of Chinese Competitive Advantage*. She lives in Shanghai.

Kaui Hart Hemmings has written three novels: *The Descendants, The Possibilities,* and *How to Party with an Infant*.

Bob Hicok, a professor at Purdue University, is the author of several collections of poetry, including *The Legend of Light*.

Robin Wall Kimmerer, a mother, botanist, and writer, is the director of the Center for Native Peoples and the Environment at the State University of New York College of Environmental Science and Forestry, Syracuse, and the author of *Braiding Sweetgrass: Indigenous Wisdom, Scientific Knowledge, and the Teachings of Plants*.

Christy K. Mack cofounded the Bravewell Collaborative, a community of philanthropists focused on integrative medicine.

Amy Maclin is *O, The Oprah Magazine*'s executive editor.

Sophie McManus has published essays and stories in *The Washington Post, American Short Fiction, Tin House*, and elsewhere, and she is the author of the novel *The Unfortunates*. She teaches writing and literature at Sarah Lawrence College.

Liza Monroy has written three books, most recently the essay collection *Seeing As Your Shoes Are Soon to Be on Fire*. She lives in Santa Cruz, California.

Catherine Newman is the author of the memoirs *Catastrophic Happiness* and *Waiting for Birdy* and the blog *Ben and Birdy*. Her first middle-grade novel will be published later this year. She lives in Amherst, Massachusetts, with her family.

Robin Romm has published a memoir, *The Mercy Papers*, and a collection of stories, *The Mother Garden*, and is the editor of *Double Bind: Women on Ambition*. She lives in Portland, Oregon.

Sasha Sagan is a writer and filmmaker in Boston.

Brenda Shaughnessy, author of the poetry collections *So Much Synth* and *Our Andromeda,* teaches at Rutgers University–Newark and lives in Verona, New Jersey, with her husband, son, and daughter.

Susanna Sonnenberg has published two memoirs, *Her Last Death* and *She Matters: A Life in Friendships.* She lives in Missoula, Montana.

Rachel Starnes is the author of a memoir, *The War at Home: A Wife's Search for Peace (And Other Missions Impossible).*

Leesa Suzman, a former beauty editor at several magazines, is now a freelance writer and editor in Scarsdale, New York.

Tracy Young is a writer and editor in New York City.